FINGER LICKIN'
FOOD

FINGER LICKIN' FOOD

Healthy family recipes from the American South

Jamie Deen

with Andrea Goto and Brianna Beaudry

Photography by John Kernick

Kyle Books

This book is dedicated to Moose and Bear and the 5 o'clock girl, with all my love.

First published in Great Britain in 2014
by Kyle Books
192–198 Vauxhall Bridge Road
London SW1V 1DX

www.kylebooks.com

10 9 8 7 6 5 4 3 2 1

ISBN 978-0-85783-245-0

Text © 2013 by Jamie Deen
Photography © 2013 by John Kernick
Book design © 2013 by Kyle Cathie Ltd

Project editor Anja Schmidt
Designer Louise Leffler
Photographer John Kernick
Food and prop styling Susie Theodorou
Copy editor Sarah Scheffel
Production Nic Jones, Gemma John and Lisa Pinnell

A Cataloguing in Publication record for this title is available from the British Library

Colour reproduction by ALTA London
Printed and bound in China by 1010 Printing Group Ltd

CONTENTS

FOREWORD
BY PAULA DEEN

One of life's greatest joys and heartbreaks is watching your children grow up. The hurt comes with knowing that once they go out into the world you cannot protect them like you once did – you can't bandage every scrape and wipe away every tear. You simply have to trust that you've given them as much wisdom and love as possible and watch them grow. And that's where the joy comes in: seeing what happens.

Since the day he was born, Jamie has been a constant source of joy in my life. His sharp humour and kind heart draw people in. That child has never known a stranger; he'll talk the ear off anybody who'll listen. For the longest time, I wasn't sure what Jamie would make of these gifts. Let's just say he wasn't the most goal-oriented when he was in school. He more or less just rode the waves, unsure of where he'd end up. Eventually he came home to his momma because I asked him to. I needed help starting up my first company, The Bag Lady, and I couldn't think of anyone better than my eldest son. We just about darn near killed each other in that tiny kitchen day in and day out. And when my youngest son, Bobby, joined, the three of us had to try real hard not to kill one another. One thing was clear: Jamie didn't like it. He was living my dream, not his.

Somewhere along the line, something suddenly 'clicked' and Jamie found his calling closer to home than I could've ever hoped or dreamed.

We had just opened up The Lady & Sons together when Jamie fell hard for this tall, gorgeous Southern brunette who would become my daughter-in-law. He took to marriage and his budding career with a kind of maturity that I hadn't expected. He started building the life he had always wanted.

Looking back, it shouldn't have surprised me that Jamie was ready to settle down. He had always been a natural cook and charismatic leader, and he clearly craved the loving, lasting marriage that his momma and daddy didn't have. Then, when my grandbaby Jack was born, it was game over for Jamie. He threw himself headfirst into fatherhood, putting his family before anything else. Today he has two boys who both look at their father as if he hung the moon.

In between nappy changes, T-ball games and kids' playtimes, Jamie has managed to build a successful career around food and family. He's the star of his own Food Network cooking show, *Home for Dinner*, and has now realised his dream of writing his first solo cookbook – a book that is as much about him as it is about the family who joins him at the table each and every night. Every recipe in this book has a history, many dating back generations in the Deen or Hiers families. Jamie has adapted these dishes to meet the nutritional and emotional needs of the modern family. They are full of freshness and flavour, and include locally sourced ingredients whenever possible. The recipes in this book are sure to become the ones my grandbabies will pass down to their children. And with this book, they will carry on to your family table as well.

To say that I'm proud of the cook, husband and father Jamie has become is a real understatement. While his daddy and I tried to give our best, we didn't always have the best to give. In spite of this, Jamie has managed to live his dream, which you can see, feel and taste in every page of this book.

And what a beautiful dream it is.

INTRODUCTION

Food and family. Are there any two things that more folks, regardless of background, value?

Food was the tie that bound my family together when Bobby and I were growing up and, as adults, it has literally saved us from a lifetime of instability and countless struggles.

My mom cooked a Sunday-worthy spread just about every night of the week when Bobby and I were young boys. Unbeknownst to us, this was a by-product of her agoraphobia and an inability to leave the house. Talk about silver linings. The majority of my memories from that time are of being around the table together as a family. My mom's laughter when Bobby and I both reached for the fried chicken breasts while my poor old daddy learned to like legs and thighs. The cake Mom baked for Jesus's birthday every Christmas Eve – coconut cake, the only cake I really care to eat to this day. My daddy cutting butter into cane syrup and soaking it up with white bread for dessert. Momma, a Southern sommelier, teaching us the significance of different cornbreads and how to pair them with certain foods like they were fine wines – lacy cornbread with creamed potatoes, skillet cornbread with chilli and hoecakes with collard greens and pot liquor.

My memories spread out over the many different kitchens of our extended family. My Granny Paul had a tiny kitchen in her trailer on the edge of Lee County, Georgia, USA. It wasn't even a double-wide, but the food and flavour she created there could have filled a palace. Her garden was the first soil I ever pulled food from: potatoes, squash, tomatoes and my favourite, fresh collard greens. Her neighbour Mr Carr allowed Bobby and me to pick fresh strawberries from his wondrous plants of overflowing berries. I was nine years old but remember those sweet, ripe berries like we picked them yesterday. My Great Aunt Peggy's kitchen had a built-in banquet where we ate her cucumber, onion and tomato salad. We enjoyed every meal with fresh garden veggies in oil with cider vinegar. I can taste it right now.

Family and food. You all have these memories, too.

My momma taught me that the kitchen is the heart of the home and she has never been more right. Brooke and

I have two little boys who are piling up their own food memories right now. Jack, well, just turn this book over and see how food and family are shaping his life. Matthew at 23 months is never happier than when he is in our arms at the stove. In this family you are either going to be a food lover or a 'cooker man', as Jack used to call my occupation, but most likely you're going to be both.

MY LIFE AS A COOKER MAN

My cooking experience is divided into five distinct stages. The first was as a prep cook – and I started young. When I was a boy I shelled peas 'til I thought my fingers were gonna fall off. Mom said, 'You're gonna want to eat them, so keep shelling.' With butter and fresh onions on top of white rice? Yes ma'am, I wanted to eat 'em. So I shelled and shucked and scrubbed and cleaned, building up far more memories than I did skill, which is really the point.

After this came work-for-pay. For my first job, at age 15, I was in charge of making cheeseburgers and also anointed head trash taker-outer. Of course, the job was at a used car auction house but, you know, a *nice* one. This period came to a close with my summer at Yellowstone National Park, where I cooked at the Old Faithful Inn. We were under the direction of the stoic chef Mike Dean – his memory still so fresh in my 'kitchen mind', it's like I just saw him yesterday.

Next up was the family restaurant, The Lady & Sons. We started our business on a prayer and two hundred dollars, and have grown it into so much more than that. One bright memory is the day our self-published cookbook *Favourite Recipes from the Lady and Her Friends* was ready to be picked up from the printer. Bobby and I had slipped in a surprise dedication for Mom, and when she saw it, she just cried and cried. It was such an accomplishment for her and we were all so proud. She even took an unheard-of day off to recover in bed. If you ever see a copy, check us out on the back cover – we were so exhausted, we are almost unrecognisable. So many years ago, so many memories.

A few years back, I embarked on the most surprising stage: I became a 'television cooker man'. Bobby and I spent a summer travelling the entire country together, meeting small-business owners and featuring them and their food on our Food Network programme, *Road Tasted*. Brooke was travelling with us and we were expecting Jack… it was such an exciting and memorable summer.

We've just wrapped shooting season two of another Food Network series, *Home for Dinner,* starring yours truly, but more important, my entire family is involved. There are too many memories associated with the show to list here, but being invited down to the field at Sanford Stadium to watch my beloved Georgia Bulldogs play football is at the top. Oh, and I've met three US presidents. Thanks, TV.

But after all these years, the role I have enjoyed the most is as a 'parent cooker man'. From the time Brooke began making fresh baby food, we have been on a culinary carousel of wonder. There have also been stretches of hand wringing. The wants of a hungry two-year-old are known only to said toddler and they ain't saying. What I can say with certainty is that nothing beats the show a baby can put on with spaghetti. My personal mantra – turn every challenge into a positive – has been especially useful during the first years of table food. My tried-and-true advice to new parents? Introduce your kids to as many different textures and flavours as you can dream up because there are few things worse than living stuck in a chicken nugget rut.

EATING 'GOOD' FOOD

So, here we are living in an age where 'farm to table' is packaged like a commodity. Today there is an entire industry built around this concept, which is funny because my Granny Paul just called it 'supper'. The best food I've ever eaten is the food that I've watered as its roots spread into the soft Georgia soil. We keep a small garden at home for odds and ends we are able to cultivate. I don't even own a pair of overalls, so don't let me sound like I'm talking from my high horse, or high tractor as the case may be, but growing at least some of your own food *is* gratifying. Parents barely have time to keep our zips up, so finding fresh food takes effort, but it's well worth it. We supplement our efforts by having a farm box of right-from-the-ground-or-vine seasonal produce delivered to our doorstep each week, and we make a habit of visiting the local farmers' market as a family on Saturday mornings.

Caring about what and how our boys eat has really changed my approach to food. We eat fresh, stock up on produce and avoid frying foods in our home altogether. I've also started eating like a six-year-old – rather than stuffing myself whenever the feeling strikes, I keep it to three square meals a day, made up of smaller portions. As someone who grew up wearing jeans from the plus-size section, I'm happy to tell you of an unexpected bonus of cooking in this way – the most successful weight management I've ever experienced. Eat like a six-year-old, it's good for all of us.

Whether it's a big family meal at Granny Paul's trailer park or Aunt Peggy's house or an everyday dinner in my mom's kitchen or my own, food is love. Plain and simple. If I manage to inspire my kids with this message, then I'll feel I've done right by them.

CHERISHED THINGS

Two of my most cherished things live in my kitchen. One is my Granny's skillet (frying pan), bought from Sears who knows how many years ago. It has hosted more chickens than a barnyard and its colour has faded to an orange reminiscent of the last light of a beautiful sunset. It's my museum piece. The other is one of my sweet little momma's chopping boards. My dad made it in his shop and it has been in my life as long as I can remember. It's the size of a bread plate and doesn't offer much more space than to cut a lemon, but I wouldn't trade it for a Cadillac.

This book you are now holding is a fantastic realisation of a dream for me – my new cherished item. It's also no small miracle that, after all the obstacles our family has faced and overcome, we are still just that, a family. We love each other, we encourage each other, we push and we pull for each other and we celebrate all the hard-fought victories, big and small. This book is a big one. Becoming a writer has always been the golden ring that I've reached for. Bobby and I first realised this dream together years ago when we published our Deen Bros. cookbook series. Sharing this accomplishment with my brother was one of the most special moments I'll ever experience, but this book here seems different. Bigger. That was our life and this is mine – my beautiful, blessed life that allows me to cover the food and people that I love most. And I'm very grateful to share this with y'all. So enough visiting, let's shake some pots.

FROM THE GROUND UP

From the Ground Up

The farm-to-table movement has gained a lot of ground recently, but let's not forget that people have been eating this way for generations. My grandmother Paul had it going on back in 1976 with her little garden of cucumbers, potatoes, tomatoes, lettuce and the best green beans I've ever had.

In Albany, Georgia, Mom and Dad had a really big garden – about two acres – just outside of town on Aunt Peggy and Uncle George's property. I loved being outside, running between the neatly planted rows of corn, onions and potatoes and just about every kind of lettuce you can imagine. When I got hungry, I'd pull a carrot straight from the ground, brush off the soil and eat it on the spot. Once I even dug up a perfectly intact Native American arrowhead. That garden was a pretty magical place.

The magic died down a bit when I got a little older and Bobby and I had to work the garden for a couple of summers, tilling, planting and weeding. That's when I started to realise that it was a necessity for our families; the garden was the only reason we enjoyed fresh produce on our table every single day – leafy salads, weighted down with juicy ripe tomatoes and crisp carrots. Mom would preserve just about anything she could stuff into a jar – from sweet figs to pickled watermelon rinds – so that our family could enjoy fruits and vegetables well into winter. The back-breaking work gave me an appreciation of fresh produce that I still have today.

My garden doesn't come close to the size of Aunt Peggy's, but we do have fruit trees and a small container garden where Jack and I have just started to grow carrots and peppers. Jack's responsible for keeping his plants watered and weeded, and he takes his job just as seriously as Aunt Peggy did all those years. He's even learned patience from having to wait until the tomatoes are ripe enough to pick. And when he finally does get to make a big salad with the fruits and veggies he grew, he garnishes it with his favourite toppings and is so proud of what he's created – from garden to table.

That's why I've titled this chapter 'From the Ground Up'. Every recipe starts with something simple – chopped lettuce, chunks of watermelon, a bed of rice or even crackers – and then incorporates lots of fresh vegetables and herbs. The end result is a set of flavourful, kid-pleasing recipes that reinvent the typical 'garden salad', transforming it into the highlight of your family table.

AUTUMN HARVEST SALAD WITH MAPLE VINAIGRETTE

Serves 4–6

Prep Time: 15 minutes
Cook Time: 30 minutes

Making the perfect salad is like walking a tightrope – it's all about balance, marrying contrasting colours, textures and sweet and savoury flavours. The roasted butternut squash gives this salad a beautiful deep-orange colour and toothsome texture, while the grapes sweeten things up. The same goes for the dressing: Dijon mustard, maple syrup and red wine vinegar – each contributes a unique kick; together they're a full-on roundhouse. By adding salty feta, which is Brooke's favourite, and pistachios, Jack's nut of choice, there's something to lure everyone to the table.

1 small butternut squash (about 675g), peeled, deseeded and diced

2 tablespoons olive oil

sea salt and freshly ground black pepper

215g mixed baby salad leaves

1/2 head radicchio, thinly sliced

1 head chicory, thinly sliced

150g seedless red grapes, sliced in half

75g feta cheese, crumbled

60g salted roasted pistachio nuts, chopped

MAPLE VINAIGRETTE
(MAKES ABOUT 120ML)

1/2 small shallot, very finely chopped

2 tablespoons red wine vinegar

1 tablespoon real maple syrup

1 teaspoon Dijon mustard

3 tablespoons olive oil

sea salt and freshly ground black pepper

Preheat the oven to 200°C/gas mark 6.

Place the butternut squash on a baking tray and drizzle with the oil. Season with salt and pepper and toss it all together. Roast for 30 minutes, giving the squash a good flip halfway through to ensure that it cooks evenly. Leave to cool to room temperature.

Meanwhile, make the maple vinaigrette. Put the shallot, vinegar, maple syrup, Dijon, olive oil and salt and pepper in a glass jar with a tight-fitting lid. Shake well to combine; taste and adjust the seasoning.

After the squash has cooled, get yourself a large serving bowl and combine half of the butternut squash (reserve the rest for another use or nibble on it while you're prepping the salad), the mixed leaves, radicchio, chicory, grapes, feta and pistachios. Drizzle with the maple vinaigrette and toss it all together real well. Serve it up immediately.

COOKING TIPS

If your kids are adverse to sharp flavours, serve up their salad at the table before mixing in the bitter radicchio and chicory.

When Jack moved on to table food, Brooke would roast butternut squash, put it through a food processor, pour it into ice-cube trays and then freeze it so we'd always have some on hand.

Before I started cooking with butternut squash, I'd see it in the grocery store and think it was a Thanksgiving decoration. Who eats a gourd? Well, I guess I do.

Broccoli is really versatile; you can eat it raw, mashed, grilled or even fried. You can cover it with melted cheese or toasted almonds. It also makes for the perfect tree in your child's kindergarten diorama.

Broccoli is one of my favourite vegetables and that's probably what turned Jack and Matthew on to it. But people tend to fall into a rut when they prepare broccoli, making it the same way they always have: steamed with butter. What we're going to do here is make a colourful salad that's as easy to prepare as it is to pack up and carry on a picnic. The fresh crunch from the broccoli, beans, apple, celery and sunflower seeds pairs perfectly with the sweet, sour and smoky flavour of the bacon vinaigrette, giving this salad a flavour profile as rich as a good bottle of wine.

CRISP BROCCOLI SALAD WITH BACON VINAIGRETTE

Serves 4–6

Prep time: 20 minutes
Cook time: 10 minutes

Bring a large saucepan of salted water to the boil. Add the beans and cook for 2 minutes, then add the broccoli and cook for a further 1–2 minutes until the broccoli is bright green and tender-crisp. Transfer to a colander and run the veggies under cold water until completely cool. Pat dry with a clean tea towel and transfer to a large serving bowl along with the apple, celery, sunflower seeds and cranberries.

Meanwhile, cook the bacon in a medium sauté pan for about 5 minutes until the fat is rendered and the bacon is crisp. Using a slotted spoon, transfer to a kitchen paper-lined plate. Pour off about 1 tablespoon of the bacon fat. Add the shallot and sauté over a medium heat for about 1 minute until soft. Turn off the heat and quickly whisk in the Dijon, vinegar and brown sugar. Drizzle the salad with the dressing, add the reserved bacon, toss it really well and season with salt and pepper.

COOKING TIP

The key is not to overcook the broccoli – that's the only way you can really mess it up. It literally only takes a minute to boil it. As soon as it turns bright green, pull it out.

150g frozen shelled soya (edamame) beans

600g broccoli florets

1 Gala apple, or other sweet, crisp apple, peeled, cored and chopped

2 celery sticks, sliced

65g salted roasted sunflower seeds

30g dried cranberries

sea salt and freshly ground black pepper

BACON VINAIGRETTE

5 smoked streaky bacon rashers, chopped

1 medium shallot, finely chopped

1 teaspoon Dijon mustard

80ml red wine vinegar

1 tablespoon soft light brown sugar

JACK'S FAVOURITE PASTA SALAD WITH LOADS OF VEGGIES

Serves 6

Prep Time: 5 minutes
Cook Time: 15 minutes

you can use whatever pasta you like, but we often go with wagon wheels because they're Jack's favourite. I'm good with it as long as he doesn't think it's hilarious to roll 'em across the table during dinnertime.

This dish gets more play at our house than any other recipe in the book because it's easy and everybody loves it. We'll have it once a week as a main course without fail. It's so satisfying – it's like I'm taking the entire food pyramid and tossing it into a bowl. This recipe's got vegetables, grains, dairy, a bit of oil, fruit (tomato counts) and you can easily add a protein such as chopped-up grilled chicken if you want. You can also exchange any of the vegetables for ones that you and your kids prefer. Sometimes I'll dress up my bowl with pine nuts or olives, while keeping my kids' dish pretty traditional. This attention to their preferences makes for a more peaceful dining experience for everyone!

350g wagon wheel (rotelle) pasta

150g frozen shelled soya (edamame) beans

2 carrots, well scrubbed and cut into 1cm chunks

350g broccoli, cut into bite-sized florets

150g baby plum tomatoes, sliced in half

115g grated firm mozzarella (pizza) cheese or fresh half-fat mozzarella, diced

3 tablespoons olive oil

2 tablespoons red wine vinegar

55g mayonnaise

1 teaspoon sugar

sea salt and freshly ground black pepper

Add the pasta to a large saucepan of boiling salted water. Cook the pasta for 3 minutes less than recommended on the back of the packet. When the timer goes off, add the beans and carrots and cook for a further 2 minutes. Next, add the broccoli and continue boiling for another minute.

Drain the pasta and veggies in a colander. Rinse really well under cold water to stop the cooking process. (Make sure you drain off all the liquid so that you don't water down your salad.) Transfer the pasta and veggies to a large serving bowl, along with the tomatoes and mozzarella.

Put the oil, vinegar, mayonnaise, sugar and salt and pepper in a glass jar with a tight-fitting lid and shake it until it's all mixed up. Taste and adjust the seasoning.

Pour the dressing over the pasta, toss well and serve warm, though you can make ahead if you need to.

BARBECUED RAINBOW CHOPPED SALAD

Serves 6

Prep time: 10 minutes
Cook time: 10 minutes

Remember the days when the only people who ate salads were skinny girls who complained they were fat? Back then salads were a punishment. At best, they were used as a stall tactic as you waited for the meal you actually wanted. But over the years, we've all come to realise that there's so much more to salad than a head of iceberg lettuce. In fact, this recipe is the best example of what a salad should aspire to be: full of colour, flavour and texture. And because I still get to work the barbecue, no one questions my manhood when I want a salad for dinner.

1 medium courgette, sliced in half lengthways

1 medium orange pepper, sliced into quarters

1 small red onion, sliced into 1cm-thick rings

2 corn on the cobs, husked

2 tablespoons olive oil

sea salt and freshly ground black pepper

150g baby plum tomatoes, sliced in half

1 large ripe avocado, stoned, peeled and diced

10g fresh basil leaves, torn

1 Cos lettuce heart, chopped

40g baby rocket

LEMONY DIJON DRESSING

2 teaspoons Dijon mustard

juice of ½ lemon

3 tablespoons extra-virgin olive oil

sea salt and freshly ground black pepper

Heat an outdoor gas barbecue to medium-high or heat a griddle pan on the hob over a medium-high heat.

Place the courgette, orange pepper, onion and corn on a baking tray, drizzle with the oil and season with salt and pepper. Add the veggies to the barbecue or griddle pan and cook them for 8–10 minutes, rotating so that all sides are evenly cooked. Remove and let them sit just until they're cool to the touch. Chop the courgette, pepper and onion into bite-sized pieces and cut the corn kernels off the cobs. Transfer the chopped vegetables to a large serving bowl. Add the tomatoes, avocado, basil, lettuce and rocket.

To make the dressing, put the Dijon, lemon juice, olive oil and salt and pepper in a glass jar with a tight-fitting lid and shake well to combine; taste and adjust the seasoning. Pour your dressing over the salad and toss it together. Serve immediately.

OLD-FASHIONED CRACKER SALAD

Serves 6

Prep Time: 10 minutes
Cook Time: zero

This 'salad' is probably the craziest-sounding recipe that you'll find in this book, but you've got to try it. Trust me, it's like egg salad on steroids. We used to make this for our packed lunches back when we had The Bag Lady because it was so easy to throw together. You're literally making something out of nothing. The few ingredients it calls for are things most people already have on hand: crackers (I use traditional American Saltines), tomatoes, celery, onions, mayonnaise and eggs. The result is a creamy side salad that pairs especially well with soup or a sandwich at lunchtime and Oven-fried Haddock Fillets (page 116) at dinner. Your friends and family will never guess what they're eating, and I promise you that they'll never forget this dish, either – for all the right reasons.

Break up the crackers by hand in a medium bowl to get a nice chunky texture. Add the rest of the ingredients, mix well and serve immediately.

115g Saltine crackers, or use Doria Doriano Italian crackers or Ritz crackers

1 plum tomato, finely chopped

2 celery sticks (including leaves), diced

4 spring onions, finely chopped

225g mayonnaise

4 hard-boiled eggs, finely chopped

The only way you can screw this up is by letting it sit too long. Its lifespan is 10-15 minutes. I mean, it's mayonnaise on crackers.

WATERMELON, FETA AND MINT SALAD

Serves 6

Prep time: 15 minutes
Cook time: zero

My cousin introduced me to dipping carrots in yellow mustard, which sounds real weird, but tastes surprisingly good. This salad definitely falls into the 'mustard-on-a-carrot' category.

Watermelon, onion, feta and mint may seem like a strange flavour combination, but then you taste it and wonder why you ever questioned it. Besides being super-pretty – the white feta and green mint pop against the pink of the watermelon flesh – it's a perfectly light and refreshing dish that you can take to a baby shower or picnic. And you don't have to bother with leftovers; Brooke always comes home with an empty bowl.

$1/2$ small red onion, thinly sliced

2 tablespoons rice wine vinegar

2 tablespoons sunflower or rapeseed oil

sea salt and freshly ground black pepper

$1/2$ deseeded watermelon (1.8kg), peeled, sliced or cubed

50g feta cheese, crumbled

15g fresh mint leaves, torn

Place the onion in a large serving bowl and drizzle with the vinegar and oil; season with a big pinch of salt and pepper. Toss everything together and let the onion marinate for 5 minutes so that it softens and loses some of its bite. Then add the watermelon, feta and mint and toss really well. Serve immediately.

COOKING TIP

You don't want to make this salad too far ahead of time. I suggest serving it immediately after you dress it, or the watermelon will start to get slimy. If transporting, bring your tossed onions and watermelon, mint and feta separately and toss together on site.

SOUP KITCHEN

Soup Kitchen

Soups and stews have always been a big part of my family's cooking. When I was a kid, Mom made them because they were easy, affordable and always yielded a ton. We'd happily eat soup for a couple of days because it would get better and better the longer it stayed in the fridge. Her chicken and rice soup rarely lasted more than two days because we loved it so much, but if it did, Mom would freeze the leftovers in small containers for quick, go-to lunches.

I've always been a chilli and beef stew kind of guy – the heartier the soup, the better – and if I were still a single guy, these would be all that I'd cook. But thank goodness Brooke came along and introduced me to things like grooming products, tumble dryer sheets and the goodness of lighter soups. You can really see her influence in this chapter. While I still include recipes like Creamy Roasted Broccoli Soup and my World's Best Chilli (which is guaranteed to win in any cook-off), Brooke encouraged me to develop a number of lighter recipes with just as much flavour, including Kale and White Bean Soup and, her personal favourite, Brooke's Easy Egg-drop Soup.

Like my mom, I take great joy in cooking my family a big, comforting pot of soup that takes four hours to slow-cook on the hob, but I just don't have that kind of time during the week. So, all of the recipes in this chapter take very little time to prepare and yet they taste delicious. If you still crave a simmer-all-day soup, just follow Mom's advice and make extra to store in the freezer where the flavours can sit and marry together for up to six months. Now that's love.

GINGERY BUTTERNUT SQUASH BISQUE

Serves 6

Prep time: 15 minutes
Cook time: 35 minutes

An added bonus: if this soup does end up on the ceiling, it will clean up rather nicely.

Proof that butternut squash has a flavour with universal appeal. It was the first solid food both my boys ate – and liked. I know, because it didn't end up on the ceiling. So, we've served butternut a lot of different ways in our house. This soup is one of my favourites because it packs so many sweet and savoury flavours into every spoonful. The fresh ginger gives this creamy soup a touch of heat that's balanced by the sweetness of the apple. It makes for a satisfying weeknight meal, although it could just as easily hold its own at a dinner party. (After having kids we never actually host dinner parties, but I just know it would be great.)

2 tablespoons olive oil

1 medium onion, chopped

2 garlic cloves, chopped

5cm piece fresh ginger, peeled and chopped (about 2$\frac{1}{2}$ tablespoons)

$\frac{1}{4}$ teaspoon ground cinnamon

good pinch of freshly grated nutmeg

sea salt and freshly ground black pepper

1 litre Homemade Chicken Stock (page 205)

240ml apple juice

240ml water

1 large butternut squash (1.3kg), peeled, deseeded and cut into 2.5cm chunks

1 Granny Smith apple, peeled, cored and chopped, plus more cut into matchsticks and tossed in lemon juice for serving (optional)

sour cream for serving (optional)

Heat the oil in a large saucepan over a medium-high heat. Once it's hot, add the onion and cook, stirring, for about 3 minutes until tender. Stir in the garlic and ginger, and continue cooking for a further 2 minutes until real fragrant. Sprinkle in the cinnamon, nutmeg and salt and pepper, and continue cooking and stirring for about another minute. Pour in the stock, juice and water, and bring to a good simmer. Add the squash and apple, and bring to the boil. Reduce the heat to a simmer and cook over a medium heat for about 30 minutes until the squash is tender.

Transfer the soup to a blender, in batches, and purée until smooth. Return the soup to the pan you started with and bring it back up to a low simmer. Serve in warm bowls, with a small dollop of sour cream swirled in for added creaminess, if you like.

COOKING TIP

Kid-appeal aside, this is an elegant soup that would do just fine at a special-occasion table. It looks very pretty with some sour cream swirled into the bowl and topped with apple matchsticks tossed in lemon juice to stop them turning brown, or go the extra mile and sprinkle the soup with crumbled goat's cheese.

ROASTED TOMATO SOUP WITH CHEESE CROUTONS

Serves 6–8

Prep time: 5 minutes
Cooking time: 1 hour 5 minutes

Drowning cheese croutons in soup is my grown-up way of eatin' like a kid.

Making tomato soup that comes right out of a can is fine, and believe me, there have been a few hurry-up-and-eat nights when I've done just that. But it can't compete with this roasted tomato version made from scratch. I add a squeeze of my favourite local honey and a sweet Vidalia onion that's grown just about an hour from us here in Savannah, Georgia. These fresh ingredients give the soup layers of flavour that you just can't find in a can. The cheese croutons came about as a kind of compromise. I'm a 'dunker' – I use a sandwich instead of a soup spoon – but Brooke can't stand soggy bread. So I serve her croutons on the side and sprinkle mine on top.

1.3kg plum tomatoes, cut in half

1 sweet onion, cut into quarters

6 garlic cloves, smashed but not peeled

3 tablespoons olive oil

1 tablespoon honey

sea salt and freshly ground black pepper

1 litre Homemade Chicken Stock (page 205)

1 tablespoon chopped fresh dill,
plus more for serving

Cheese Croutons (recipe follows)

COOKING TIP

Roasting the tomatoes brings out their natural sweetness and adds depth of flavour. The honey kicks up the sweetness a notch.

Preheat the oven to 220°C/gas mark 7.

Place the tomatoes, onion and garlic on a heavy-based baking tray. Drizzle with the oil and honey and season with a good-sized pinch of salt and pepper. Toss everything together with your hands and roast in the oven for 35–40 minutes, or until the tomatoes are soft and beginning to caramelise on the edges.

Slip the garlic cloves out of their skins. Using a slotted spoon, scoop the vegetables, in batches, into a blender. Purée until smooth.

Place the baking tray on the hob and add about 180ml of the stock to the pan. Scrape up any browned bits with a wooden spoon and bring the liquid to a simmer. Transfer to a large saucepan along with the remaining stock and vegetable purée. Season well with salt and pepper and simmer for 25 minutes. During the last few minutes of cooking, stir in the dill. Serve with Cheese Croutons and another sprinkle of chopped dill.

CHEESE CROUTONS
Serves 4

Prep time: 5 minutes
Cooking time: 6 minutes

4 slices sourdough bread, sliced about 1cm thick

115g mature Cheddar cheese, grated

30g butter, softened

Heat a large non-stick frying pan over a medium-high heat.

Evenly sprinkle two slices of bread with the cheese and sandwich each with a second slice of bread. Butter the outsides of each sandwich and cook for about 3 minutes per side until golden and crisp on both sides. Remove from the pan and leave to rest for 1 minute before cutting with a serrated knife into 5cm-square croutons.

BROOKE'S EASY EGG-DROP SOUP

Serves 3–4

Prep time: 5 minutes
Cook time: 15 minutes

This soup is something Brooke always orders when we go out for Chinese and I was surprised how easy it is to make at home. Like any hot soup, it's literally a great warm-up to a meal, especially if it's accompanying a dish from the same family, geographically speaking, like a stir-fry or Asian-style Tuna Burger (page 56). Or bulk up this soup by adding a few handfuls of baby spinach, chopped leftover chicken and shelled peas or soya (edamame) beans to the broth, turning a first course into a main one.

1 litre Homemade Chicken Stock (page 205)

2.5cm piece fresh ginger, thinly sliced

1 teaspoon reduced-salt soy sauce

$1/8$ teaspoon ground white pepper

1 tablespoon cornflour

2 medium eggs, lightly beaten

2 spring onions, thinly sliced

Combine the stock, ginger, soy sauce and pepper in a medium saucepan over a medium-high heat. Bring to the boil, then reduce the heat to medium and simmer for 10 minutes. Remove the ginger with a slotted spoon and discard.

Whisk the cornflour with about 60ml of the hot broth in a small bowl until smooth. Pour the cornflour mixture into the pan of simmering stock, all the while whisking. In about a minute, the broth should thicken up. Turn off the heat and swirl the broth with a wooden spoon to create a whirlpool effect, then slowly pour in the eggs. The eggs will cook in about a minute. Stir in the spring onions just before you're ready to sit down to eat.

INGREDIENT NOTE

Don't be turned off by the cornflour in the soup. It thickens up the soup to add a bit of viscosity.

DAD'S CAULIFLOWER, BEER AND CHEDDAR SOUP

Serves 4–6

Prep time: 10 minutes
Cook time: 25 minutes

Savannah hosts the second-largest St Patrick's Day celebration next to New York City, so there are plenty of 'potlucks' to prep for. When made with Guinness and Irish Cheddar, this soup is like a pot o' gold.

Back in the day, when Brooke and I could try new restaurants without considering how they ranked on the kid-friendly meter, we went to a place that served a Cheddar and beer dip that we both fell hard for. If we could've put a straw in that dip without anyone noticing, I think we would have. I got to thinking about how I could turn that dip into something we could slurp down without getting strange looks. So I took one of my favourite soups – cauliflower – and introduced beer and Cheddar flavours to create a thick, rich soup we both would enjoy. The straw's optional.

55g butter

1 medium onion, chopped

1 celery stick, chopped

1 carrot, peeled and chopped

sea salt and freshly ground black pepper

3 tablespoons plain flour

1 litre low-salt or Homemade Chicken Stock (page 205)

240ml beer or dry stout

1 medium head cauliflower (about 675g), cored and chopped

1 tablespoon Dijon mustard

1 teaspoon hot sauce

115g extra-mature Cheddar cheese, grated

Melt the butter in a large, heavy-based saucepan. Once it's foamy, add the onion, celery and carrot and sauté for about 3 minutes until tender. Season with some salt and pepper and sprinkle the flour over the vegetables. Cook, while stirring, for 2 minutes.

Whisk in the stock and beer and bring to the boil, then reduce the heat to a simmer and then add the cauliflower. Simmer for 15 minutes until the cauliflower is super-tender.

Remove from the heat and stir in the Dijon and hot sauce. Transfer the soup to a blender, in batches, and purée until velvety smooth. Return the soup to the pan and bring it back up to a low simmer. The final step is to stir in the Cheddar cheese by the handful, making sure each addition is melted and smooth before putting in more.

COOKING TIP

If you're looking for a lower-calorie soup, this recipe is surprisingly delicious even without the cheese.

Sadly, the parsnip has been treated like a second-class carrot for too long. I've been putting it in dishes that traditionally call for carrots and the result is a spicy, amped-up flavour in an otherwise classic recipe.

A big pot of stew always makes for a perfect family meal because it's savoury, satisfying and easy to throw together. I consider this dish a foundation recipe because you can use it to create a number of different meals, experimenting with the ingredients you have on hand. For example, this velvety full-bodied stew is really good over rice or as a filling for a puff pastry pasty. Or you can put it in a baking dish and top with puff pastry, transforming this recipe into a delicious pie.

HEARTY BEEF STEW WITH ROASTED PARSNIPS AND POTATOES

Serves 6

Prep time: 20 minutes
Cook time: 3 hours 5 minutes

Cook the bacon in a large, flameproof casserole dish over a medium heat, stirring, for about 4 minutes until nice and crisp. Using a slotted spoon, transfer to a kitchen paper-lined plate. Pat the beef dry with kitchen paper and season with salt and pepper on all sides. Add 2 tablespoons of the oil and the beef to the casserole, in batches, and brown well on all sides. Transfer to a large plate.

Add the onion and garlic to the casserole and cook for about 5 minutes until the onion is just beginning to turn golden brown. Sprinkle in some salt and pepper, then stir in the tomato purée. Cook for 2 minutes, then stir in the stock and vinegar. Add the bay leaf and thyme and return the beef to the casserole. Bring the stew up to the boil, then reduce to a simmer, cover with a lid and cook for a good 2½ hours until the beef is fork-tender, stirring on occasion.

About an hour before the beef has finished cooking, preheat the oven to 200°C/gas mark 6. Place the parsnips and potatoes on a baking tray and drizzle them with the remaining 2 tablespoons oil. Season with salt and pepper and roast for 35–40 minutes until browned and tender, flipping with a spatula halfway through cooking. Just 5 minutes before serving time, remove the bay leaf and stir the roasted parsnips and potatoes into the stew.

INGREDIENT NOTES

Braising steak is great for stews. It's a tough cut of meat with lots of connective tissue that melts when cooked low and slow. Look for red meat that's marbled with fat. While I like the subtle spicy flavour the parsnips provide, feel free to roast your family's favourite root vegetables.

4 smoked streaky bacon rashers, cut into 1cm pieces

900g braising steak, trimmed of visible fat and cut into 4cm cubes

sea salt and freshly ground black pepper

4 tablespoons olive oil

1 large sweet onion, chopped

4 garlic cloves, smashed

175g canned or jarred tomato purée

1 litre low-sodium or Homemade Chicken Stock (page 205)

1 tablespoon balsamic vinegar

1 bay leaf

4 fresh thyme sprigs

3 parsnips, cut into 2.5cm chunks, halved if thick

450g medium Yukon Gold or Maris Piper potatoes, well scrubbed and quartered

KALE AND WHITE BEAN SOUP

Serves 6

Prep Time: 10 minutes
Cook Time: 40 minutes

This chunky soup is a perfectly satisfying supper for a cold night. Hearty enough to be dinner on its own when served with a green salad and some good crusty bread.

This soup borrows from that Southern tradition, making a warm, hearty meal that's perfect for autumn – or, as I prefer to call it, football season. But unlike heavy chowders and meaty chillis, this broth-based soup is really good for you. If you haven't had much experience with kale, now is the time to get to know her. Dubbed the 'queen of greens', this close relative of cabbage could take spinach in an arm-wrestling match any day. It's one of the healthiest vegetables on the planet; 100g of kale gets you 180% of the daily requirement of vitamin A, 200% of vitamin C and a whopping 1,020% of vitamin K. Just knowing that makes me feel like I could leap over a building with a single bound.

1 tablespoon olive oil

350g turkey sausages, casings removed

1 medium onion, finely chopped

2 garlic cloves, finely chopped

350ml Homemade Chicken Stock (page 205)

1 x 400g can chopped tomatoes

1 x 400g can cannellini beans, drained and rinsed

sea salt and freshly ground black pepper

1 bunch kale, tough stems removed, leaves chopped into 1cm pieces

freshly grated Parmesan cheese for serving

crusty bread for serving (optional)

Heat the oil in a large saucepan over a medium-high heat. Once it's hot, add the sausage meat and cook for 3–4 minutes until browned, stirring and breaking up the meat as best you can with the back of your spoon.

Add the onion and sauté for just about 3 minutes until tender. Stir in the garlic and sauté for a further 1–2 minutes until the aromas really start to come out. Pour in the stock, tomatoes with their juices and beans, and season it all with a big pinch of salt and pepper. Bring the soup to a simmer, then stir in the kale by big handfuls. Simmer over a medium heat for 30 minutes, stirring on occasion.

Serve each bowl topped with some Parmesan cheese along with some crusty bread to sop up the goods.

INGREDIENT NOTE

Kale can be a bitter woman. If you prefer a milder flavour, opt for smaller leaves. Either way, look for firm, deeply coloured leaves with hardy stems.

WORLD'S BEST CHILLI

Serves 6–8

Prep time: 15 minutes
Cook time: 2 hours 15 minutes

I've been a judge at more than my share of chilli cook-offs, so I know that everybody's got their secret this or that to make a prize-winning stew. But honestly, I've yet to taste one that beats the recipe I came up with about 15 years ago. I was asked to do a cooking demonstration for a wonderful organisation called The Living Vine, which assists expectant mothers who are facing some real challenges in their lives. I decided to teach the women how to make chilli; since most of the ingredients come from a can, it's simple and inexpensive, but also incredibly satisfying. The recipe was so popular that they published it on their website and named it 'The Living Vine Chilli'. To this day, I still get calls from people who've won competitions with that recipe.

2 tablespoons olive oil

1 large red onion, diced

2 medium peppers (green and red), diced

2 celery sticks, diced

5 garlic cloves, chopped

675g lean beef mince

4 tablespoons chilli powder

1 tablespoon ground cumin

1 tablespoon dried oregano

$^1/_2$ teaspoon cayenne pepper

175g canned or jarred tomato purée

2 x 400g cans chopped tomatoes

400g sunblush tomatoes, drained and diced

350ml beer

2 x 400g cans red kidney beans, drained and rinsed

1 x 400g can pinto beans, drained and rinsed

grated Cheddar cheese for serving (optional)

sour cream for serving (optional)

chopped spring onions for serving (optional)

Heat the oil in a large, flameproof casserole over a medium-high heat. Once the oil is hot, add the onion, peppers and celery and sauté for about 4 minutes until soft. Add the garlic and sauté for 1–2 minutes just until fragrant. Stir in the mince, breaking it up with the back of your wooden spoon, and cook for about 5 minutes until browned. Stir in the chilli powder, cumin, oregano and cayenne and sauté for about a further 2 minutes. Stir the tomato purée into the beef; this will intensify the flavour. Add all the tomatoes, the beer and all the beans, stirring to combine. Bring the chilli to the boil, then reduce to a simmer, cover with a lid and cook over a medium-low heat for a good 2 hours, stirring on occasion to keep the chilli from sticking to the bottom of the pan.

If you like, top each bowl with grated Cheddar, sour cream and chopped spring onions before serving.

COOKING TIP

One of the best things about making a big pot of chilli is that you can freeze the leftovers. All the flavours will continue to marry together, so it'll be even better when you reheat it.

This version here includes one of my favourite ingredients, beer.

SUPER-SIMPLE LEMON CHICKEN AND RICE SOUP

Serves 8

Prep time: 10 minutes
Cook time: 30 minutes

I'm surprised to see how many people turn to a can for comfort food. When the sniffles hit you, the last thing you want is a runny, colourless concoction of condensed anything. Instead, take just a few extra minutes (literally) to cook up a bowl of this homemade chicken and rice soup. The lemon juice gives it a bright, zesty flavour. It'll cure you, guaranteed.

2 tablespoons olive oil

1 medium onion, finely chopped

2 large carrots, peeled and cut into half-moons

sea salt and freshly ground black pepper

1 litre Homemade Chicken Stock (page 205)

475ml water

juice of 2 lemons (about 120ml)

90g long-grain rice

1 bay leaf

300g leftover cooked chicken, chopped

2 tablespoons chopped fresh parsley

Heat the oil in a large saucepan over a medium-high heat. Once it's hot, add the onion and carrots and sauté for about 4 minutes until tender. Season with salt and pepper and pour in the stock, water and lemon juice. Bring it all to the boil, then stir in the rice, add the bay leaf and knock down the heat to a simmer. Cook for 20 minutes until the rice and carrots are tender. Stir in the chicken and cook for just a few minutes longer until the chicken is heated through. Sprinkle in the parsley and give a taste for seasoning, adding salt and pepper if it needs it. Remove the bay leaf before serving.

CREAMY ROASTED BROCCOLI SOUP

Serves 4–6

Prep time: 15 minutes
Cook time: 35 minutes

With just a little bit of olive oil and a dash of salt and pepper, roasted vegetables have a sweet, full-bodied taste that will trump boiled veggies any day. So here I've taken that fantastic flavour and turned it into a smooth and creamy broccoli soup – it's one of Brooke's favourites. What you lose in colour during roasting, you'll more than make up in flavour.

about 800g broccoli

1 medium onion, chopped

3 tablespoons olive oil

sea salt and freshly ground black pepper

350ml Homemade Chicken Stock (page 205)

2 tablespoons freshly grated Parmesan cheese

120ml double cream

grated Cheddar cheese for serving (optional)

Preheat the oven to 220°C/gas mark 7.

Trim the broccoli and chop the stems into 1cm pieces; cut the top into bite-sized florets. Place the broccoli and onion on a rimmed baking tray and drizzle with the oil. Season with salt and pepper and toss it all together. Roast for 20–25 minutes until the broccoli is cooked through and golden brown in spots, tossing halfway through.

A few minutes before the broccoli is finished roasting, bring the stock up to a simmer in a medium saucepan. Add the broccoli to the simmering broth and cook for 10 minutes to allow the flavours to marry together.

Transfer the soup to a blender, in batches, and purée until it's really smooth. Return the soup to the pan and bring to a low simmer. Stir in the Parmesan cheese and cream. Serve in bowls and sprinkle with some grated Cheddar, if you like.

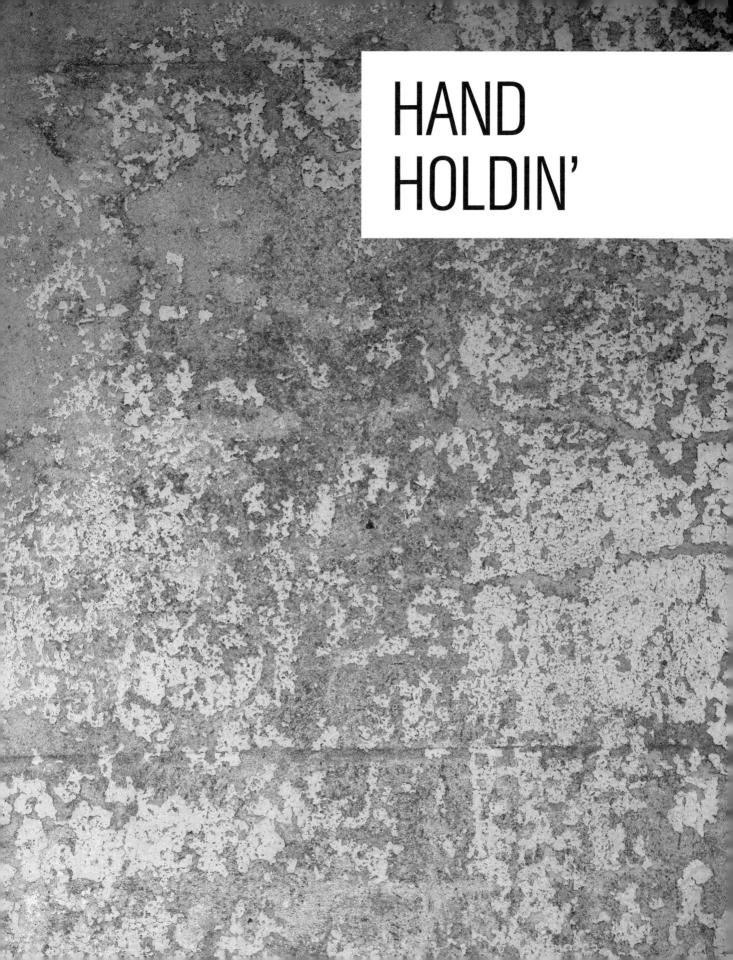

HAND
HOLDIN'

Hand Holdin'

I've been in the food industry for more than 25 years, and as a result, I can sear a steak and supreme an orange with the best of 'em. But I'm still that guy who finds certain domestic tasks a little tedious – such as making my bed and washing dishes. I'm only going to be out of that bed for a few hours and I'm going to use a plate and fork at least three times a day, so I feel like I'm constantly tidying up, just to mess things up again. It's not that I'm lazy – quite the opposite. I'm a married man with a restaurant to run, a TV show to shoot and a million commitments in between. Add in two kids and a bulldog with respiratory challenges and life starts to get real crazy, real fast.

Enter the sandwich. The sandwich is God's gift to anyone who's constantly on the run. The washing-up is minimal; the portability maximised. I'm actually able to eat with one hand and make work calls, play with action figures and clean up dog drool with the other.

I was first introduced to the art of the sandwich back in college, when I spent a summer working at Yellowstone National Park in Wyoming. A buddy and I worked in the pantry kitchen at the Old Faithful Inn, where all we did was make soups and sandwiches for the two million people who went through the park. I'd have a ham sandwich for breakfast just as often as I'd have one for lunch, just because it was so quick and simple.

Surprisingly, I never tired of sandwiches and it's a good thing, because by the time I returned from Yellowstone, Momma was set to launch The Bag Lady, where we bagged around 250 sandwiches a day. We started off with the basics – ham, turkey and egg salad sandwiches. It was good, simple food that was no trouble to make. But as the business started to boom, Mom got inspired, putting things like grilled chicken and Boston pork butt (shoulder) on homemade buns – and the rest is history.

The recipes in this chapter are a reflection of my long-standing affair with the sandwich. They run the gamut, from the Four Pillars (page 63), which were the foundation for The Bag Lady, to more contemporary and complex fare like Asian-style Tuna Burgers (page 56) and Southwestern Turkey Clubs with Chipotle Mayo (page 52). Every recipe comes with a homemade topping that takes something ordinary – like mayo and coleslaw – and transforms it into something extraordinary when it's loaded onto these fork-free dishes. Plates optional. Napkins required.

HOMEMADE BLACK BEAN BURGERS WITH FRESH PICO DE GALLO

Makes 4 burgers

Prep time: 20 minutes
Cook time: 20 minutes

A very satisfying veggie burger. I like having them for leftovers for lunch, too. Just a quick reheat in the microwave and your lunch is ready to go.

If you would've told me 20 years ago that I'd eat – and enjoy – a black bean burger, I would have slapped you round the face with a quarter pounder. Black bean burgers were for sorority girls, not a meat eater like myself. I was reintroduced to black beans while working in our restaurant, where we served them with crab cakes. I spent many a day hunched over the stove, tweaking the seasoning so that the beans had just enough bite without overpowering the crab cakes. These black bean patties are a twist on my mom's old recipe. Growing up, she'd make us what she called bean-cake sandwiches. Come to think of it, she made cakes out of just about anything – corn, black-eyed peas (beans), butter (you've gotta try her Gooey Butter Cake) – so I guess it's only natural for me to make a savoury bean sandwich for my boys as well. I've added soya (edamame) beans to the mix for a pop of green and topped it all off with homemade Fresh Pico de Gallo, which is sure to earn Jack and Matthew some future points from the sorority girls . . .

4 tablespoons olive oil

$1/2$ small red onion, finely chopped

1 large carrot, peeled and diced

3 garlic cloves, very finely chopped

1 tablespoon chilli powder

$1/2$ teaspoon smoked paprika

sea salt and freshly ground black pepper

2 x 400g cans black beans, drained and rinsed

115g frozen shelled soya (edamame) beans, defrosted

1 medium egg, beaten

4 soft wholemeal hamburger buns, toasted

sour cream for topping

Fresh Pico de Gallo (recipe opposite)

Heat 2 tablespoons of the oil in a large non-stick frying pan over a medium heat. Once the oil is hot, add the onion and carrot and cook for about 4 minutes until softened. Stir in the garlic, chilli powder and paprika, and continue cooking for a further 1 minute. Season the mixture with a big pinch of salt and pepper. Toss in the black beans and soya (edamame) beans and give it all a good stir. Remove the bean mixture from the heat and scrape it into a bowl; leave it all to cool to room temperature.

Once it's cool, transfer the bean mixture to a food processor. Give it a good pulse, but make sure it stays chunky (you don't want it to be smooth). Stir in the egg and season lightly with salt and pepper. Press the mixture into four 10cm patties.

Wipe your frying pan clean with some kitchen paper, then heat the remaining 2 tablespoons oil in it over a medium heat. Once it's hot, add the patties, reduce the heat to medium and cook for about 5 minutes on each side just until they're browned and crisp. Sandwich the burgers on the toasted buns and top with the sour cream and Pico de Gallo.

FRESH PICO DE GALLO

Combine all of the ingredients together in a mixing bowl and season with 2 big pinches of salt. Leave the Pico de Gallo to stand at room temperature for about 20 minutes to really get the flavours to marry before serving.

To me, coriander tastes like soap. But if you are a fan of that squeaky-clean flavour, feel free to add some.

Makes about 675g

Prep time: 20 minutes
Cook time: zero

6 plum tomatoes, diced (about 675g)

1 garlic clove, very finely chopped

1 small mild green chilli, deseeded and finely diced

1/2 small red onion, finely diced

1 1/2 teaspoons olive oil

finely grated zest and juice of 1 lime

sea salt

SOUTHWESTERN TURKEY CLUBS WITH CHIPOTLE MAYO

Makes 2 sandwiches

Prep time: 15 minutes
Cook time: 15 minutes

Here, I've downsized the original club so you can actually get your mouth around it, but if you want to double stack, that's your call.

The traditional turkey club sandwich seems to be a featured item on just about every golf-club menu across the country. I had this Southwestern version when I was in California – and true to form, that sandwich was stacked as high as my handicap and held together by four cocktail sticks working overtime. It's the perfect sandwich because it includes so many textures and flavours – it's got the pickled jalapeños, the creamy pepper cheese, and homemade Chipotle Mayo, which gives plain ol' mayonnaise a kick in the pants. (The guacamole and Little Gem lettuce keep the heat in check.)

8 smoked streaky bacon rashers

10 smoked turkey slices (from the deli counter)

4 slices nice white bread, toasted

4 Cheddar slices with cracked black pepper or Monterey Jack cheese slices

1 plum tomato, sliced

2 tablespoons jarred sliced green jalapeños

4 leaves Little Gem lettuce

Chunky Guacamole (page 62)

CHIPOTLE MAYO

1 tablespoon drained and chopped canned chipotle chillies

115g mayonnaise

sea salt and freshly ground black pepper

Preheat the oven to 200°C/gas mark 6.

Arrange the bacon on a foil-lined baking tray and cook in the oven for 18–20 minutes, or until crisp. Drain on a kitchen paper-lined plate.

Meanwhile, make the chipotle mayo. Mash the chillies, mayonnaise and salt and pepper to taste together in a small bowl until smooth.

Divide the turkey between two slices of bread, layering each with two rashers of bacon and two slices of cheese. Top with the tomato slices, jalapeños and lettuce. Spread the remaining two slices of bread with the chipotle mayo, then the guacamole. Close up each sandwich and slice in half for serving.

BLACKENED FRESH CATCH SANDWICHES WITH EASY TARTAR SAUCE AND PICKLED RED ONIONS

Makes 4 sandwiches

Prep time: 5 minutes
Cook time: 10 minutes

Taking the time to pickle red onions and make my own tartar sauce gives this sandwich a fresh homemade flavour that you're just not going to find when throwing a piece of fish on a baguette. To taste the difference, take the time to do something different – and by 'time' I mean 15 minutes, tops. Tilapia, red snapper or grouper would all work here.

1 tablespoon sea salt

2 teaspoons freshly ground black pepper

1 teaspoon cayenne pepper

2 teaspoons smoked paprika

2 teaspoons garlic powder

4 x 175g river cobbler (or tilapia, red snapper or grouper) fillets

2 tablespoons rapeseed oil

Tartar Sauce (recipe right)

4 small (20cm) sesame baguettes or long crusty rolls (hoagie rolls to us), split and toasted

Pickled Red Onions (recipe right)

1 small avocado, stoned, peeled and thinly sliced

30g baby rocket or 55g iceberg lettuce, shredded

Whisk together the salt, pepper, cayenne, smoked paprika and garlic powder in a small bowl. Generously sprinkle both sides of the fish with the spice mixture.

Heat a large cast-iron frying pan over a medium-high heat. Add the oil and, once it's hot, add the fish fillets and cook for about 4 minutes on each side until blackened and cooked through.

Spread tartar sauce on both sides of the baguette halves. Place the blackened fish fillets on the bottom half of each baguette and top with the pickled red onions, avocado slices and rocket or shredded lettuce. Cover with the baguette top halves and serve.

TARTAR SAUCE
Makes about 280g

Prep time: 5 minutes   Cook time: zero

225g mayonnaise

60g pickled cucumber relish

1 tablespoon lemon juice

dash of hot sauce

sea salt and freshly ground black pepper

Mix together all the ingredients in a small bowl. Season with salt and pepper to taste. The sauce can be stored in the refrigerator in a covered container for up to 1 week.

PICKLED RED ONIONS
Makes about 500g

Prep time: 5 minutes   Cook time: 5 minutes

350ml cider vinegar

50g sugar

$1/2$ teaspoon sea salt

1 bay leaf

1 small dried chilli

1 medium red onion, sliced

Combine the vinegar, sugar, salt, bay leaf and chilli in a medium saucepan and bring to the boil. Stir the vinegar mixture until the sugar is dissolved, then add the onion and reduce the heat to a simmer. Cook for 5 minutes until the onion is softened. Turn off the heat and leave the contents to cool in the saucepan. To store, transfer to a preserving jar and refrigerate for up to 1 month.

INGREDIENT NOTE

Pickled red onions will last a month in the refrigerator. Chop them up and add to various recipes that need a kick, such as green salads, grains or sauces.

ASIAN-STYLE TUNA BURGERS WITH PICKLED GINGER MAYO AND CHINESE LEAF SLAW

Makes 4 burgers

Prep time: 20 minutes
Cook time: 10 minutes

Here's my Asian twist on an American classic: the hamburger. After I transform tuna steaks into a beef mince consistency in the food processor, I make them into the lightest and leanest patties you can imagine and sear them for just a few minutes on each side. A quality tuna burger like this calls for some fancy accompaniments that'll make plain old pickles and mayo blush. I garnish mine with cucumbers to give texture and crunch. Southerners love their mayonnaise; here I get the best of both worlds by seasoning it with my favourite Asian flavours – ginger, soy sauce and Sriracha hot chilli sauce. The Chinese Leaf Slaw is a fresh, cool complement to the tuna burger whether you put it on the side or under the bun. Altogether, the Asian burger, sauce and side make for a triple treat.

675g tuna steaks
1 tablespoon very finely chopped fresh ginger
2 garlic cloves, very finely chopped
1 spring onion, very finely chopped
1 teaspoon toasted sesame oil
sea salt and freshly ground black pepper
1 tablespoon rapeseed oil
Pickled Ginger Mayo (recipe opposite)
4 soft hamburger-style buns, toasted
cucumber slices for serving
Chinese Leaf Slaw (recipe opposite)

Cut the tuna into 2.5cm cubes. Add half to the bowl of a food processor and pulse about 12 times, or until finely chopped; be careful not to overprocess it. Scrape the tuna into a mixing bowl and repeat with the remaining tuna. Fold the ginger, garlic, spring onion and sesame oil into the tuna, and season with salt and pepper. Form into four equal-sized patties, about 10cm in diameter. Transfer the patties to a plate, cover with clingfilm and refrigerate for about 20 minutes to firm them up.

Heat the rapeseed oil in a non-stick frying pan over a medium heat. Add the burgers to the hot pan and cook for just 3 minutes on each side. Spread Pickled Ginger Mayo on each toasted bun, add a tuna burger, top with cucumber slices and sandwich between the buns. Serve with the Chinese Leaf Slaw – either on top of the patty or alongside.

INGREDIENT NOTE

We're only using a small amount of Sriracha and chilli here, but if your kids are averse to any kind of heat, just leave them out.

 ## COOKING TIP

If you're feeling lazy, you can save yourself some knife work by pulsing the ginger, garlic and spring onions in a food processor; transfer it to the mixing bowl before adding the tuna. A food processor is a busy cook's friend.

PICKLED GINGER MAYO
Makes about 115g

Prep time: 5 minutes   Cook time: zero

115g mayonnaise
2 tablespoons finely chopped pickled ginger
1 teaspoon Sriracha hot chilli sauce
½ teaspoon soy sauce

Combine all your ingredients in a small bowl. The mayo can be made up to 3 days ahead. Store in the refrigerator in a tightly covered container.

CHINESE LEAF SLAW
Makes about 450g

Prep time: 20 minutes   Cook time: zero

2 tablespoons lime juice
1 tablespoon rice wine vinegar
1 tablespoon sesame oil
1 tablespoon rapeseed oil
1 teaspoon sugar
½ head Chinese leaf, shredded (about 150g)
1 red pepper, thinly sliced into matchsticks
1 carrot, well scrubbed and grated
2 spring onions, thinly sliced
½ small green chilli, deseeded and thinly sliced (optional)
sea salt

Whisk together the lime juice, vinegar, sesame oil, rapeseed oil and sugar in a mixing bowl. Add the Chinese leaf, red pepper, carrot, spring onions and chilli, if using, and toss all together. Season with a big pinch of salt.

Sriracha, or the 'red rooster' as we call it, is a staple in my house. It goes on everything, including my chicken salad.

LAZY-DAY PULLED PORK SANDWICHES WITH SLAW

Serves 6–8

Prep time: 10 minutes (plus overnight marinatin')
Cook time: 5-7 hours

If I have the opportunity to really mess around when making dinner, I like to smoke my pork butts (shoulders). But if I'm really busy, I pull out the slow cooker. I can get the pork cooking in the morning, and seven hours later, I come home and it's done. It's a delicious way to enjoy a traditional-tasting pulled pork sandwich on busy weeknights. No matter how I prepare it, I eat pulled pork the same way every time – with a big scoop of coleslaw on top. This recipe is for a coleslaw that's always been in our family; it's my favourite version because I leave out what I don't like – mainly peppers. I also like my coleslaw a little sweeter, so I put in some sugar and cider vinegar to balance out the bite of the onion and cabbage. It's not super-creamy, but it doesn't need to be – the barbecue sauce takes care of that. This simply gives you another dimension of flavour and texture to a sandwich that, by nature, is blessed.

SPICE RUB

2 tablespoons sea salt

2 tablespoons soft light brown sugar

1 tablespoon paprika

1 teaspoon smoked paprika

1 teaspoon garlic powder

1/2 teaspoon ground cumin

1/2 teaspoon chilli powder

1/2 teaspoon celery seeds

1.8kg whole pork shoulder on the bone (the US cut known as Boston pork butt)

Jamie's Tangy BBQ Sauce (page 92)

sea salt

6–8 buns

Creamy Tangy Coleslaw (recipe opposite)

The night before you want to make your sandwiches, mix together all the rub ingredients in a small bowl. Rub the spice mixture on to cover the entire pork joint, including all the nooks and crannies. Place the pork on a large plate, cover with clingfilm and refrigerate overnight so that all the flavours blend together and really infiltrate the pork.

The next morning, transfer the pork to a slow cooker and add 250g of BBQ sauce. Cover with the lid and cook over a low heat for 7 hours, or high heat for 5 hours, until the pork is extremely tender.

Remove the pork from the slow cooker, leaving the cooking liquid behind, and place in a large bowl. Shred the pork with tongs or two forks. Drizzle in 60ml of the BBQ sauce, sprinkle with a big pinch of salt and toss it all together. Serve the pulled pork on buns, topped with the coleslaw and additional barbecue sauce.

COOKING TIP

Both the pork and the slaw taste a whole lot better if you leave them to marinate overnight.

INGREDIENT NOTE

Boston butt is a great cut of meat from the shoulder of a hog. It's generally inexpensive, serves a ton of people and if cooked correctly always juicy, tender and melt-in-your-mouth delicious.

If I'm not feeling like bread, I'll just put baked beans in a bowl, layer on the pulled pork and coleslaw and eat it all together like it's a barbecue cocktail . . . if it were in a much smaller container.

CREAMY TANGY COLESLAW
Serves 6–8

Prep time: 15 minutes (plus 1 hour marinatin')
Cook time: zero

1 small head (900g) green cabbage, thinly sliced

1 large carrot, peeled and shredded

3 tablespoons finely chopped red onion

130g mayonnaise

3 tablespoons cider vinegar

1 tablespoon sugar

2 teaspoons yellow mustard

1 teaspoon celery seeds

sea salt and freshly ground black pepper

Simply toss all of the ingredients together in a medium bowl, cover with clingfilm and leave to marinate in the fridge for at least 1 hour or overnight before serving.

CHICKEN SANDWICH WITH BACON, SWISS CHEESE AND CHUNKY GUACAMOLE ON GRIDDLED BREAD

Makes 2 sandwiches

Prep time: 10 minutes
Cook time: 20 minutes

This is a brilliant way to use up leftover roasted chicken.

This is Brooke's all-time favourite sandwich at Uncle Bubba's Oyster House, so we do it on the barbecue at home a lot. I've found that adding bacon and guacamole transforms a 'ho-hum' chicken sandwich into something you'll have dreams about. We use avocados a lot because the boys love 'em. In fact, I've found that they will roll their sleeves up for anything I put guacamole on – it's kind of like how you can get a dog to take a pill by hiding it in a cube of cheese.

4 smoked streaky bacon rashers

4 slices nice crusty sourdough bread

55g butter, at room temperature

150g cooked chicken, roughly chopped

4 Swiss Gruyère cheese slices

1/2 beef tomato, thinly sliced

CHUNKY GUACAMOLE

1 large ripe avocado, stoned and diced

3 tablespoons very finely chopped red onion

1 tablespoon sour cream

1 tablespoon lime juice (about half a lime)

sea salt

Preheat the oven to 200°C/gas mark 6.

Place the bacon on a foil-lined baking tray and bake for 10–12 minutes, or until crisp. Transfer to a kitchen paper-lined plate to drain.

Meanwhile, make the guacamole. Coarsely mash the avocado, onion, sour cream and lime juice together in a mixing bowl. Season with a big pinch of salt and set aside.

Heat a griddle pan over a medium-high heat. Spread both sides of the bread slices with the butter and cook for about 2 minutes per side until crisp and golden grill marks appear. Divide the chicken between two slices of the bread, then layer each with the bacon and cheese. Return the sandwiches to the griddle pan and cover with a domed lid for 1–2 minutes just until the cheese is melted. Carefully remove the lid and remove the sandwiches from the pan.

Top your sandwiches with the tomato slices. Spread the remaining two slices of bread with the chunky guacamole and close up each sandwich. Slice them in half for serving.

INGREDIENT NOTE

Guacamole is a great alternative to mayonnaise. It has the same satisfyingly creamy texture but it's colourful and good for you. In this version, keeping it a little chunky makes it seem even more filling – plus, I don't like to skimp. This recipe makes about 175g, enough for several sandwiches.

THE FOUR PILLARS

In 1989, my mom called me up to tell me that she was starting a business and needed my help. She was going to sell packed lunches. I pictured her wandering into school cafeterias, finding the kids whose mothers couldn't find their way around a kitchen and selling them a sandwich for 50 cents – not exactly the road to riches. I wasn't too far off. In the beginning, Mom would get up before the sun and make around 50 sandwiches. At lunchtime, she wanted me to drive them over to the Medical Arts Building where she had worked. There, I'd sell packed lunches to her friends, who preferred the home-cooked taste of Mom's sandwiches to the bag of crisps stuffed in their desk drawers that they often scarfed down between appointments.

She didn't ask for help, she *told* me I was going to help. Reluctantly, I showed up to work, not because I was excited about the venture (I wasn't), but because I didn't have much else going on. I had finished college and was let loose into the world without any real sense of where I was headed, so home seemed like as good a prospect as any. At least I was guaranteed a meal, which was better than the majority of my college days.

I was as charismatic as any 20-something, basket-carrying, sandwich-peddling kid could be, but Mom's business was really built around four pillars: pimento cheese (see Bits and Pieces, page 207, for my perfected take on this recipe), chicken, tuna and egg salad sandwiches.

I had grown up on those lunches, so at first I didn't realise what all the fuss was about. Eventually I realised what I'd taken for granted all those years – Mom could really cook.

She didn't do anything fancy. She made honest, straightforward meals that people liked. That people were willing to pay for. It was the most basic equation. And as much as I resented her business at the time, it taught me the value of simple food, made well, which is why my first solo cookbook – and my life – wouldn't be the same without the Four Pillars, presented here as I like to serve them. But feel free to sandwich them between slices of your favourite bread.

EGG SALAD

Serves 4

Prep time: 10 minutes
Cook time: zero

In Louisiana, they refer to onion, pepper and celery as the 'Holy Trinity'; that's the cook-down basis for every gumbo, jambalaya or *grillade* that they make. But in Georgia, the Holy Trinity is chicken salad, tuna salad and egg salad – with egg salad as the daddy of them all. And here again you'll see that I've managed to sneak bacon into my egg salad recipe to give it a salty, savoury, divine finish. So please, show some respect.

6 hard-boiled eggs, peeled and
coarsely chopped (see Cooking Tip)

4 smoked streaky bacon rashers, cooked crisp and crumbled

75g mayonnaise

60g pickled cucumber relish

1 tablespoon roughly chopped fresh dill

1 teaspoon Dijon mustard

sea salt and freshly ground black pepper

celery sticks for serving (optional)

Mix together the eggs, bacon, mayonnaise, relish, dill, Dijon and salt and pepper in a medium bowl. Serve with celery sticks, if you like.

 ## COOKING TIP

The answer to the egg-peeling conundrum: cook your eggs in water seasoned with a bunch of salt. As soon as the water boils, cover the pot and turn off the heat; let it sit for 10 minutes and your eggs are done. Peel them under running water. Now go forward and prosper, young Jedi.

TUNA SALAD

Serves 4

Prep time: 5 minutes
Cook time: zero

Tuna salad on soda crackers is one of my favourite snacks. You won't even dirty a fork.

Layers of flavour from the onion, lemon juice and sweet relish transform your run-of-the-mill tuna-and-mayo combination into something special. Look back to the Egg Salad recipe (page 63) for my perfect egg-peeling method.

2 x 185g cans tuna steak in spring water, drained

2 hard-boiled eggs, peeled and finely chopped

75g mayonnaise

juice of half a lemon

3 tablespoons thinly sliced chives

1 celery stick, finely chopped

1 tablespoon sweet relish or gherkin relish

1 tablespoon finely chopped red onion

sea salt and freshly ground black pepper

mixed salad leaves (optional)

toasted sourdough or wholemeal bread (optional)

Mix together the tuna, eggs, mayonnaise, lemon juice, chives, celery, relish and onion in a mixing bowl. Season the salad with a big pinch of salt and pepper and stir to combine. Serve on a bed of salad leaves or on toasted bread, if you like.

CHICKEN SALAD

Serves 6

Prep time: 10 minutes
Cook time: zero

Chicken Salad is something we've made our whole lives. It was one of the 'trio salads' we made religiously at The Bag Lady. But for our 'high-end' items on Fridays, we'd barbecue the chicken for the salad. Or, rather, Dad would. He'd go out at like 5 o'clock in the morning to barbecue the chicken and later we'd pick that poultry clean. Barbecued chicken salad sandwiches would fly out of our hands at a whopping $5 a pop. That's a whole lot of sandwiches when you consider how far we've come since The Bag Lady.

75g mayonnaise

1 tablespoon lemon juice

3 spring onions, finely chopped

sea salt and freshly ground black pepper

450g cooked chicken, chopped

150g red seedless grapes, sliced in half

65g toasted walnuts, chopped

6 beef tomatoes for serving (optional)

Whisk together the mayonnaise, lemon juice, spring onions and salt and pepper in a medium bowl, then fold in the chicken, grapes and walnuts. Taste and adjust the seasoning.

To serve in the tomatoes, slice off the tops. Use a paring knife to cut around the inside of the tomatoes, then use a spoon to scoop out the pulp and discard it. Season with salt and pepper, then fill with the chicken salad for serving.

 COOKING TIP

We love to serve this salad in a hollowed-out tomato for an interesting presentation – and that's one less bowl to wash.

BY LAND

By Land

I've never been a hunter. Growing up, I think I saw *Bambi* one too many times to ever be able to shoot a deer – or any creature for that matter. Dad took Bobby and me bird hunting back when I was in the fifth or sixth grade. It was fun at first – tracking the birds, sneaking up on 'em and taking aim. But what came after didn't sit so well with either one of us. The Deen boys didn't have the heart for hunting – or maybe we had too much heart to ever enjoy it.

The truth is, I've always felt that if you do hunt, you should eat what you shoot, and I don't eat game enough to justify hunting it. Today I enjoy shooting skeet out at this beautiful, private gun club in Savannah, Georgia – one of the oldest in the country. Wednesday is 'Men's Night' and it's probably the busiest time of the week. Nobody gets hurt except a flying clay disc, and, after a few high-fives with my buddies, I can head home to a roast chicken with a big appetite and a clear conscience.

We were fortunate that beef, chicken and pork were always a staple on our table when I was growing up. But don't feel as if you're limited by just three kinds of meat. Each one is available in so many different cuts. When it comes to chicken, there are legs, thighs, wings and breast meat. Some red meat is more marbled; some has less fat. There are just as many different cuts of pork: you can get a pork chop, fillet or ribs, just to name a few. The point is, if you take the time to learn about the different cuts, you'll discover a wide variety of distinct textures, flavours and possible preparations to keep you from getting stuck in a rut.

I still cook meat most days of the week, but it's less about quantity now – no more elbowing my brother out to get the last rib – and more about the quality of the preparation and presentation. Certain dishes, like a savoury roast beef fillet or a sweet and salty maple-glazed ham, can pretty much stand on their own, but I like to play with flavour pairing. The addition of white wine and leeks to One-pot Chicken and Rice (page 76) blows the lid off this traditional dish, in much the same way that a sausage and herb stuffing cranks up the appeal of an already delicious pork fillet. But nothing in this chapter outshines Brooke's Meatloaf (page 85). Now *that* I'm willing to bet Bambi's life on.

SUNDAY ROAST CHICKEN WITH SEASONAL VEGETABLES

Serves 4

Prep time: 15 minutes
Cook time: 1 hour 10 minutes

I use my Granny Paul's skillet (frying pan) for this dish. It becomes more seasoned every time I use it, making it the most seasoned pan in the history of humankind.

Sundays are the only day of the week when my family doesn't have a full slate of errands and events: no school, soccer games or birthday parties in bouncy castles that'll inevitably lead to an emergency-room visit. That means I'm able to plan and prepare this favourite family meal. A roast chicken falls right in line with relaxed Sundays – even though it takes a while to cook, it's not labour-intensive and it's a beautiful dish that's both affordable and healthy. The preparation is always the same, but I change the vegetables with the season. Whichever vegetables you prefer, the essence from the chicken seasons them all to create one delicious dish.

COOKING TIP

Save the leftover chicken carcass for Homemade Chicken Stock (page 205).

Take the chicken out of the refrigerator and pat it dry with kitchen paper. Let the chicken stand at room temperature for about 1 hour.

Very finely chop the leaves of 1 sprig of rosemary. Mix together the butter, chopped rosemary and garlic in a small bowl. Rub the chicken with the herb butter, making sure to spread some under the skin. Season the cavity of the chicken with salt and pepper, and add 1 sprig of rosemary. Liberally season the buttery outside of the chicken with salt and pepper.

Preheat the oven to 240°C/gas mark 9 and adjust the shelf to the centre of the oven.

Toss your vegetables and remaining rosemary sprig with the oil in a large roasting tin or ovenproof frying pan, and season with salt and pepper. Make sure the vegetables are well coated with the oil – they should look glossy.

Place a roasting rack over the vegetables and put the chicken on the rack, or just lay the chicken over the veggies. Roast for 20 minutes until the skin is nice and browned, then knock the heat down to 200°C/gas mark 6 and roast for a further 50–75 minutes, depending on if the chicken is on a rack or on the veggies, until a thermometer inserted into the thickest part of the thigh reads 74°C and the juices run nice and clear. Transfer the chicken to a chopping board and leave to rest for 15 minutes.

Meanwhile, using a slotted spoon, transfer the vegetables to a serving bowl. Cover them loosely with foil to keep warm. Place the roasting tin or frying pan on two burners over a medium heat. Add the stock and use a wooden spoon to scrape up the delicious browned bits on the bottom of the pan. Reduce the liquid by about half, or until the pan juices coat the back of a spoon. Be sure to add any of the juices that may have accumulated from the resting chicken.

Carve the chicken and serve with the roasted vegetables and the pan juices.

1 chicken, about 1.8kg

3 sprigs of fresh rosemary

45g butter, at room temperature

1 garlic clove, very finely chopped

sea salt and freshly ground black pepper

seasonal vegetables (see Ingredient Notes)

3 tablespoons olive oil

120ml Homemade Chicken Stock (page 205)

INGREDIENT NOTES

I always use a variety of vegetables with roast chicken based on what's fresh and in season. Here are some suggestions:

AUTUMN/WINTER

1 King Edward potato (350g), well scrubbed and cut into 4cm cubes

1 sweet potato (350g), peeled and cut into 4cm cubes

2 swedes, peeled and cut into 2.5cm cubes

2 parsnips, well scrubbed and cut into 2.5cm pieces

1 large red onion, cut into 6 wedges

SPRING

450g salad potatoes, sliced in half

1 bunch radishes, well scrubbed, tops removed

2 large leeks, dark green tops and outer layer removed, sliced in half lengthways just below the root

2 medium carrots, well scrubbed and sliced into 2.5cm pieces (thick ends cut in half)

A comforting Sunday dinner never sounded so easy . . . or tasted so good.

This dish takes me way back to when Bobby and I were just boys. It's an affordable recipe, which is why my mom made it. We may not have had ski lessons or European holidays growing up, but we always had first-rate meals. Momma's dumplings were always homemade, so these are too. If you don't have the time, you can get some shop-bought ones and drop 'em in, but I'm telling you, they're really simple to do. Everyone has their version of a dumplin' – Japan has gyoza, Italy has gnocchi and Poland has pierogi – but it all boils down to a ball of dough. It can have a filling or special ingredients mixed into the dough, but I like my dumplings plain and simple: flour, salt and water.

MOMMA'S CHICKEN AND DUMPLINGS

Serves 6

Prep time: 30 minutes
Cook time: 1 hour 20 minutes

Combine the chicken, onion, celery, carrots, thyme, bay leaves, salt and peppercorns in a flameproof casserole dish. Cover with water and bring to the boil. Reduce the heat to low and simmer gently for 45 minutes, or until the chicken is completely cooked through and tender.

Meanwhile, make the dumpling dough. Combine the flour and salt in a large bowl. Gradually sprinkle in the water, mixing it with your hands, until the dough comes together. Dump the dough onto a lightly floured surface and knead it together into a disc. Sprinkle the dough lightly with additional flour and roll it out to a 3mm thickness. Leave the dough to rest for 30 minutes.

When the chicken is done, transfer to a large plate to cool. Once it's cool enough to handle, shred the meat from the chicken with a fork, discarding the skin and bones. Strain the broth and discard the remaining solid pieces. Bring the broth back up to a simmer and reduce for about 10 minutes until you have 1.9 litres.

Using a pizza cutter, slice the dough into 2.5cm squares. Drop the squares into the simmering broth. Gently shake the casserole dish back and forth so that the dumplings don't stick together. Simmer for 5–6 minutes until the dumplings are cooked through and float to the top of the broth. Gently stir in the shredded chicken, reduce the heat to low and simmer for a further 15–20 minutes until the soup thickens.

1 chicken, about 1.6kg, quartered

1 large onion, roughly chopped

4 celery sticks, roughly chopped, plus the leaves for serving

2 carrots, peeled and roughly chopped

8 sprigs of fresh thyme

2 bay leaves

1 tablespoon sea salt

1 teaspoon black peppercorns

2.4 litres cold water

DUMPLINGS

250g plain flour, plus more for dusting

1 teaspoon sea salt

180ml cold water

COOKING TIP

Although Mom may not reduce her broth, I've found it's a surefire way to amp up the flavour. But I'm not gonna tell her that.

CRISPY PARMESAN CHICKEN CUTLETS WITH ROCKET AND AVOCADO

Serves 4

Prep time: 15 minutes
Cook time: 15 minutes

Let's not kid ourselves; sometimes one cutlet just won't cut it. In that case, double down.

Universally speaking, most kids love chicken nuggets and our boys are no exception. That said, Brooke and I just can't get behind processed deep-fried-then-frozen nuggets, let alone the kind that come in unnatural shapes. I'm good with pasta being formed into wheels or letters, but dinosaur-shaped nuggets? Not so much. We've found that cooking chicken cutlets on the hob with a bit of oil after dredging them with Parmesan and panko – a Japanese style of breadcrumbing that's lighter and crispier than a thick batter – produces a fresh and delicious alternative to processed prehistoric nuggets. Here we serve them on a bed of baby rocket, along with slices of creamy avocado, which is also a big hit in our house.

2 boneless, skinless chicken breasts, 250g each

sea salt and freshly ground black pepper

65g plain flour

2 medium eggs, beaten

110g panko breadcrumbs

35g Parmesan cheese, finely grated

1 teaspoon finely grated lemon zest

160ml rapeseed oil

140g baby rocket

1 large ripe avocado, stoned and sliced into wedges

juice of ¹/₂ lemon (about 2 tablespoons)

1 tablespoon olive oil

lemon wedges for serving

Lay the chicken breasts out on a chopping board. Hold your knife parallel to the board and slice a breast in half so that one breast is now two cutlets. Repeat with the second breast. Lay the cutlets between two sheets of clingfilm and pound with a meat mallet to a 5mm thickness. Season the cutlets on both sides with salt and pepper.

Arrange three plates in front of you. Add the flour to the first and the beaten eggs to the second. Combine the panko, Parmesan, lemon zest and salt and pepper in the third.

Dredge each cutlet first through the flour, then the egg and finally the panko mixture. Arrange on a clean tray. Refrigerate for 1 hour.

Preheat the oven to 200°C/gas mark 6.

Heat the rapeseed oil in a large non-stick frying pan over a medium heat. Once it's hot, add the cutlets, in two batches, and cook for about 3 minutes on each side until golden brown on the outside and cooked through. Transfer to kitchen paper to drain and season with salt straight after they come out of the pan. Transfer the cutlets to a baking tray and keep in the warm oven while you cook the second batch.

Place the rocket and avocado in a large bowl. Drizzle with the lemon juice and olive oil, and season with salt and pepper. Toss it all together really well and divide the salad between four plates. Top each salad with a cutlet, place a lemon wedge on each plate and serve immediately.

COOKING TIP

If your child isn't a fan of rocket's unique flavour, you can opt for baby spinach or a milder lettuce.

ONE-POT CHICKEN AND RICE WITH LEEKS AND GREEN OLIVES

Serves 4

Prep time: 10 minutes
Cook time: 1 hour 5 minutes

In this fancied-up version of old-fashioned chicken and rice, I've added leeks, green olives and white wine – ingredients more likely to appear in a fine-dining restaurant than in a weekday dish. But in this case, fancy still means affordable and satisfying because the foundation is rice and chicken thighs – which I prefer to use in this recipe because they tend to be juicier than white meat.

2 tablespoons olive oil

900g boneless, skinless chicken thighs
(about 8 thighs)

sea salt and freshly ground black pepper

2 leeks, rinsed well, trimmed and sliced
crossways

4 garlic cloves, chopped

2 plum tomatoes, chopped (about 225g)

120ml white wine

120ml water

185g white long-grain rice

115g green olives, pitted and coarsely chopped

2 tablespoons chopped fresh parsley leaves
for serving (optional)

Heat the oil in a large flameproof casserole dish or heavy, high-sided frying pan over a medium-high heat. Season the chicken thighs on both sides with salt and pepper. Once the oil is hot, brown the chicken, in batches, for 3 minutes per side until golden. Transfer to a platter and set aside.

Reduce the heat to medium. Add the leeks and sauté for about 5 minutes until soft, scraping up any browned bits from the base of the pan once the leeks release their water.

Add the garlic and cook for 1–2 minutes until fragrant, stirring. Add the tomatoes and cook about a further 4 minutes, stirring occasionally, until softened and the leeks and tomatoes melt into each other. Pour in the wine and water and stir to combine. Add the reserved chicken thighs and any juices that may have accumulated on the plate. Cover the pan with a lid, turn the heat to medium-low and cook for 25 minutes.

Transfer most of the chicken to a platter and then stir in the rice and olives, making sure the rice is completely submerged in liquid. Return the chicken to the pan, nestling the thighs into the rice and cooking liquid. Cover and cook for 30 minutes until the rice is tender and the liquid has been absorbed, rotating the pan throughout cooking.

Turn off the heat and allow the rice to steam for 5 minutes before serving. Fluff the rice with a fork. I like to serve this in bowls, with chopped parsley on top.

COOKING TIP

Make sure you clean the leeks really well. I'll even let them soak in a bowl of iced water for a few minutes so I can be sure they're super-clean. There's nothing worse than a good meal ruined by gritty leeks!

BUTTERMILK OVEN-FRIED CHICKEN

Serves 4

Prep time: 10 minutes
Cook time: 45 minutes (plus 1 hour marinatin')

Southerners know better than anyone how to fry a chicken. I don't mean to go against my raising here – because I will be the first to admit that nothing will ever replace fried chicken – but this baked version is pretty darn good. The panko, Japanese breadcrumbs that you can find at many supermarkets, forms a satisfying, crispy shell around the meat, which stays perfectly moist. It's a healthier alternative and much easier to wash up – a double bonus for parents everywhere.

1 chicken, about 1.6kg, cut into 8 pieces
(use wings for another recipe)

2 teaspoons sea salt

1 teaspoon freshly ground black pepper

1 teaspoon garlic powder

$\frac{1}{8}$ teaspoon ground thyme

350ml buttermilk

4 tablespoons hot sauce

2 tablespoons Dijon mustard

1 teaspoon paprika

170g panko breadcrumbs

2 tablespoons melted butter

Season the chicken pieces with the salt, pepper, garlic powder and thyme. Place the chicken on a plate, cover with clingfilm and refrigerate for 8 hours. (If you're in a hurry, leave the chicken to stand at room temperature for 1 hour.)

Whisk together the buttermilk, hot sauce, Dijon and paprika in a large mixing bowl. Add the seasoned chicken to the bowl, making sure it's fully covered with the buttermilk mixture. Cover and refrigerate for 1 hour.

Preheat the oven to 200°C/gas mark 6. Place a roasting rack inside a rimmed baking tray and spray it with non-stick cooking spray.

Season the breadcrumbs with salt and pepper and whisk together in a medium baking dish. Remove the chicken pieces from the buttermilk, letting the excess drip off, then dredge them through the breadcrumbs one at a time, patting the crumbs to the chicken to adhere. Evenly space the chicken pieces on the rack and lightly drizzle with the melted butter. Bake for 45 minutes until the chicken is cooked through and the breadcrumbing is golden brown.

MAPLE-GLAZED CHRISTMAS HAM

Serves 15–20

Prep time: 5 minutes
Cook time: up to 5 1/2 hours

This Christmas ham is a tradition that my mom passed down to us and I'm happy to share it with y'all. Even after a big Christmas breakfast with Brooke's parents, I still have room for Mom's ham at dinnertime. The Dijon combined with the brown sugar and syrup creates such a beautiful glaze and boasts an incredible flavour that plays perfectly against the ham's saltiness. The knuckle end is attractive plus a little less fatty with more meat than the fillet end. Serve with Creamy Potato Gratin (page 143) and Autumn Harvest Salad with Maple Vinaigrette (page 16).

1 smoked gammon joint on the bone, preferably knuckle end, about 5.5–6.8kg

MAPLE GLAZE
55g butter
4 tablespoons maple syrup
55g soft light brown sugar
2 teaspoons chopped fresh thyme
2 teaspoons Dijon mustard
sea salt and freshly ground black pepper

Preheat the oven to 180°C/gas mark 4 and move a shelf to the lower third of the oven.

Using a sharp knife, score a diamond pattern into the top and sides of the ham. Place a roasting rack in the bottom of a large roasting tin and set the ham on top. Pour 1 litre water into the bottom of the tin and cover the tin tightly with foil. Bake the ham for 20 minutes per 450g up to a maximum of 5 hours.

Meanwhile, start on the glaze. Combine the butter, maple syrup, brown sugar, thyme and Dijon in a small saucepan over a medum heat. Season with salt and pepper to taste and simmer, while stirring frequently, for 4–5 minutes. Set the glaze aside as the ham bakes.

After the main cooking time is up, remove the foil from the ham and glaze it every 5 minutes for 30 minutes, or until the ham is cooked through with an internal temperature of 71°C. Remove the ham from the oven and leave to rest for 10 minutes. Brush again with the glaze and carve.

COOKING TIP

Use the 'buddy method'. Pass time in the kitchen chatting with a friend since you're going to be anchored to the oven, glazing the ham every 5 minutes, for the last half hour of cooking.

ROAST PORK LOIN WITH SAUSAGE, FIGS AND FRESH HERBS

Serves 6

Prep time: 15 minutes
Cook time: 1 hour 5 minutes

We make this recipe a lot at home. It has the 'I slaved in the kitchen all day' look, but really takes no time at all. If you're looking for a memorable celebratory meal, the layers of flavour wrapped into this pork loin make this a surefire bet. Just be sure to have copies of the recipe to share with your guests; I guarantee they'll ask. We served it up here with some sautéed baby kale.

1 tablespoon olive oil

450g Italian recipe, Sicilian-style or Toulouse pork sausages, casings removed

3 garlic cloves, chopped

4 large fresh sage leaves, rubbed

1 tablespoon chopped fresh rosemary

1 tablespoon chopped fresh thyme

sea salt and freshly ground black pepper

200g finely chopped dried figs

60ml dry white wine

3 tablespoons chopped fresh parsley

1 boneless centre-cut pork loin, about 1.3kg

RUB

2 tablespoons olive oil

1½ teaspoons fennel seeds

1 tablespoon roughly chopped fresh rosemary

sea salt and freshly ground black pepper

Preheat the oven to 220°C/gas mark 7. Line your baking tray with foil.

Heat the olive oil in a large frying pan over a medium-high heat. Once it's hot, add the sausage meat and cook for about 4 minutes until browned, stirring and breaking it up with the back of a wooden spoon. Stir in the garlic, sage, rosemary and thyme, season with salt and pepper, then cook for a further 2 minutes until fragrant. Stir in the figs and sauté for a further 1 minute, then hit it with the white wine. Scrape up any browned bits that form on the bottom of the pan and cook for about 3 minutes until the stuffing is almost dry. Transfer to a bowl, stir in the parsley and leave to cool completely.

Next, butterfly your roast. Take a sharp knife and cut down through the centre of the loin, opening it up like a book (leave 5cm on one end, being sure not to cut all the way through). Pound the pork with a meat mallet until it's an even 4cm thickness. Season with salt and pepper. Spoon the cooled stuffing mixture down the centre of the roast, and roll it up like a Swiss roll into a tight cylinder. Tie the pork loin every 5cm with kitchen string. Transfer the tied roast onto the foil-lined baking tray.

To prepare the rub, place the olive oil, fennel seeds, rosemary and salt and pepper to taste in a mortar and grind with a pestle into a paste (you could also use a spice grinder or a coffee grinder used just for spices).

Rub the outside of the pork with the paste and season again with salt and pepper. Lay the pork, fat side up, on the baking tray and roast for 30 minutes. Lower the heat to 180°C/gas mark 4 and continue to roast for a further 25 minutes until a meat thermometer inserted into the thickest part of the meat reads 63°C. Leave the pork loin to rest for 15 minutes before slicing and serving.

Turn the page to see how to stuff and tie up the loin . . .

People are always impressed when you bother to stuff a pork loin, but really, it's just a dressed-up version of a pig in the blanket. Okay, make that a really dressed-up version.

BARBECUED PORK CHOPS WITH HONEY-ORANGE MUSTARD GLAZE

Serves 4

Prep time: 5 minutes
Cook time: 20 minutes

Because Brooke and I don't fry food in our home kitchen, I've started barbecuing my pork chops, but they have a tendency to dry out. So I came up with a really good glaze that incorporates sweet, citrus and savoury flavours and seals in the moisture, too. It's a simple summertime supper that takes less than 30 minutes, start to finish. These pork chops are awesome with the Greek Salad Couscous (page 147) or the Barbecued Rainbow Chopped Salad (page 24).

80ml orange juice

2 tablespoons honey

2 tablespoons Dijon mustard

1 tablespoon soy sauce

4 bone-in centre-cut pork chops, 2.5cm thick

sea salt and freshly ground black pepper

Heat an outdoor gas barbecue to medium-high.

Whisk together the orange juice, honey, Dijon and soy sauce in a small saucepan. Reduce the sauce over a medium heat for about 7 minutes until it's thick like maple syrup.

Season the pork chops on both sides with salt and pepper. Cook the chops on the barbecue for 5 minutes on each side, brushing both sides with the glaze during the last 2 minutes of cooking, and again just before taking them off the barbecue.

BROOKE'S MEATLOAF WITH SUN-DRIED TOMATOES AND FRESH MOZZARELLA

Serves 8

Prep time: 10 minutes
Cook time: 1 hour

Hands down, my wife's meatloaf is the best thing I've ever eaten in my life.

Brooke doesn't cook much, but when she cooks this, buddy, look out. I'll have her meatloaf for dinner and then I'll make a meatloaf sandwich for dessert. Honest to God. Brooke prefers to use sun-dried tomatoes jarred in olive oil because they're moist and flavourful. The fresh breadcrumbs add lightness, too.

1 medium onion, finely chopped

2 garlic cloves, very finely chopped

2 medium eggs, lightly beaten

100g drained sun-dried tomatoes in oil, chopped

110g fresh breadcrumbs (see Ingredient Note)

225g mozzarella cheese, finely chopped

315g Basic Tomato Sauce (page 206)

4 tablespoons chopped fresh basil

sea salt and freshly ground black pepper

900g lean beef mince

Preheat the oven to 180°C/gas mark 4. Line a baking tray with foil.

Add the onion, garlic, eggs, sun-dried tomatoes, breadcrumbs, mozzarella, 65g of the tomato sauce and basil to a large mixing bowl and give it a good stir to combine. Season the mixture with a generous pinch of salt and pepper. Add the mince, season with another pinch of salt and pepper and toss it all together with your hands just until combined. (Be sure not to overdo it or the meatloaf will be dense and heavy rather than nice and light.)

Plop the mixture down on the prepared baking tray and use your hands to form it into a loaf shape. Drizzle the top with 185g of the remaining tomato sauce and bake for 55 minutes. Drizzle the remaining 65g tomato sauce on top and cook for a further 5 minutes, for a total of 1 hour.

Remove the meatloaf from the oven and leave it to rest for 10 minutes before slicing it up and serving.

INGREDIENT NOTE

It's important to use fresh breadcrumbs here. To make them, add a chunk of baguette to a food processor and grind it up until it's a fine texture.

JACK'S PORCUPINES

Serves 4–6

Prep time: 10 minutes
Cook time: 55 minutes

This is a cute recipe that you can do for the kids, and the parents will like it as well because it's really satisfying. Basically, it's a jacked-up meatball. Bobby and I got a big kick out of it when we were growing up and I'm sure it'll make its way into your rotation of weekday go-to meals as well.

450g lean beef mince

275g white long-grain rice

50g Parmesan cheese, finely grated

1 small onion, finely diced

2 garlic cloves, very finely chopped

sea salt and freshly ground black pepper

300g canned chopped tomatoes and their juice

100g drained sunblush tomatoes, diced

500ml low-salt or Homemade Chicken Stock (page 205)

Preheat the oven to 180°C/gas mark 4. Spray a 23cm x 33cm baking dish with non-stick cooking spray.

Gently combine the beef mince, 95g of the rice, the Parmesan, half of the onion and the garlic and season with a big pinch of salt and pepper. Roll the mixture into 12 golf ball-sized meatballs.

Place the remaining 180g rice, the chopped tomatoes and their juice, sunblush tomatoes, stock and remaining onion. Season with salt and pepper and stir to combine. Add the meatballs to the dish, turning to coat them with the liquid. Cover the dish with foil and bake for 55 minutes.

Remove the foil from the top of the baking dish and admire your cute little porcupine meatballs! Serve the meatballs over the tomato rice.

RED WINE-BRAISED SHORT RIBS WITH HERBED RICE PILAF

Serves 6 (about 8 ribs per serving)

Prep time: 20 minutes
Cook time: 3 1/2 hours

Scraping browned bits is the cooking version of panning for gold. It's the way to get the most concentrated flavour you can out of a dish.

2.25kg meaty short beef ribs, trimmed of excess fat

sea salt and freshly ground black pepper

4 tablespoons olive oil

1 red onion, finely chopped

2 celery sticks, finely chopped

1 carrot, peeled and finely chopped

3 garlic cloves, smashed

2 tablespoons chopped fresh rosemary

2 tablespoons tomato purée

600ml dry red wine

600–720ml low-salt or Homemade Chicken Stock (page 205)

1 bunch fresh thyme

1 dried bay leaf

chopped fresh parsley for serving

Ribs are not a 'first date' kind of food. To get at the meat, you've got to be willing to throw yourself into it, elbows and all. Luckily, once you're married, you no longer have to suffer through awkward dinners using a tiny fork while being strangled by an overly starched shirt. You can scratch, wear comfy trousers and eat ribs with abandon. My boys already understand this – they've grown up cutting their teeth on rib bones. That's where the flavour is. I know it's common advice to select a cut of meat that's marbled with fat because it offers a lot of flavour, but that's not the case here. Because it's a bone-in rib, there's already going to be a lot of flavour even before you sauce it up.

This recipe is also a breeze to make because most of the work can be done in advance, giving you a couple of hours to enjoy that little bit of after-school time you have with the family while your ribs are cooking. And the process is even more enjoyable if you take a cue I learned from Justin Wilson, the first television chef I ever watched. Every time he poured wine into a recipe, he'd take a nip – sometimes straight from the bottle. Which leads me to another important point: you don't need a top-tier wine to cook with, nor do you want a bottom-of-the-barrel brand. Always cook with what you enjoy drinking. What's left in the bottle makes for a nice pairing and a romantic gesture – and helps my wife overlook the comfy trousers.

Preheat the oven to 160°C/gas mark 3.

Pat the short ribs dry and season them up good on both sides with salt and pepper. Heat 2 tablespoons oil in a large flameproof casserole dish over a medium-high heat. Once the oil is hot, add the short ribs, in two batches, and brown 'em really well on all sides. Each batch should take a good 15 minutes to get that nice dark brown colour. (Be patient 'cause that colour means flavour.) Remove the first batch of browned ribs to a platter and repeat with the second batch.

Drain off the fat from the pot, add the remaining 2 tablespoons oil and return to a medium-high heat. Once it's hot – and it shouldn't take long – add the onion, celery, carrot and garlic and sauté for about 6 minutes until softened and browned. Season with salt and pepper and add the rosemary. Stir in the tomato purée and brown for 3 minutes, stirring. Add the wine and 600ml stock to the pot, and scrape up any delicious browned bits from the bottom of the pot with the back of your wooden spoon. There's lots of flavour here, so be sure to get it into the sauce. Bring the mixture up to a simmer and return the ribs to the pot, making sure they are just covered with liquid, adding a bit more stock if you need to. Tie the thyme and bay leaf together using kitchen string and drop it right into the pot.

Cover the inside lid of the pot with some foil and put the lid on the pot. Place the pot in the oven for 2¹⁄₂ hours until the ribs are super-tender and the meat is about to fall off the bone. Remove the ribs to a baking dish, discarding bones if they fall off, and cover with the foil from the top of the lid to keep warm.

Place the casserole dish over a medium heat on the hob and reduce the sauce for about 10 minutes until it's thick enough to lightly coat the back of a spoon.

Serve the short ribs over a bed of Herbed Rice Pilaf (page 90). Sprinkle with chopped parsley.

INGREDIENT NOTES

When buying your short ribs, you want the meatiest ribs with the least visible fat. I like to use the sort that have been sliced across the bones, which in the USA are known as 'flanken cut'.

If you opt for a shop-bought stock to save time, you'll want to get the low-salt version. The liquid will reduce throughout the long cooking process, intensifying the salty flavour.

COOKING TIP

This is a fantastic dish for entertaining because all the work is done ahead of time. Just take the short ribs out of the pot and reduce the sauce just before your guests are ready to eat.

HERBED RICE PILAF

Short ribs are so rich that it's wise to pair them with this herbed rice pilaf. The rice offers a nice, bright contrast to the heavy sauce and meat. The combo may sound fancy, but kids love ribs and rice.

Serves 6

Prep time: 10 minutes
Cook time: 25 minutes

30g butter

1 small onion, finely chopped

1 garlic clove, smashed

sea salt and freshly ground black pepper

1 dried bay leaf

3 sprigs of fresh thyme

275g white long-grain rice

600ml Homemade Chicken Stock (page 205)

3 tablespoons roughly chopped fresh parsley

Melt the butter in a medium saucepan over a medium heat. Add the onion and garlic and season with salt and pepper. Cook, stirring occasionally, for about 5 minutes until the onion is softened. Stir in the bay leaf and thyme during the last minute of sautéeing. Add the rice and stir to coat with the butter. Pour in the stock and bring to the boil, then reduce the heat to a simmer, and cook, covered, for 15–17 minutes until the rice is tender. Leave to stand for 5 minutes, then fluff up with a fork and fold in the parsley.

INGREDIENT NOTE

Using chicken stock rather than water takes this rice up a notch. The fresh parsley gives it a little kick of colour, too. If your child's afraid of all things green, skip this step.

ROAST BEEF FILLET WITH ROSEMARY

Serves 6

Prep time: 15 minutes
Cook time: 25 minutes

I don't know how many people still put out two kinds of meat at Christmas dinner, but Momma has been doing this beef fillet alongside a ham for as long as I can remember. Even on its own, this no-fuss roast is always a showstopper – you're not gonna serve this if you've got the paper plates out.

5 tablespoons olive oil

2 garlic cloves

3 tablespoons chopped fresh rosemary, plus 2 sprigs of fresh rosemary

sea salt and freshly ground black pepper

1.1kg whole beef fillet, tied with kitchen string at every 2.5cm

CREAMY HORSERADISH SAUCE
(MAKES ABOUT 250G)

240ml sour cream

2^1/$_2$ tablespoons grated fresh horseradish or drained jarred grated horseradish in vinegar

2 tablespoons double cream

1 small shallot, very finely chopped

2 teaspoons Dijon mustard

sea salt and freshly ground black pepper

Add 3 tablespoons of the olive oil, the garlic, chopped rosemary and a big pinch of salt and pepper to the bowl of a food processor and purée until you have a nice paste. Rub the entire roast with the purée, making sure to get into every nook and cranny. Leave to stand for 1 hour at room temperature to take off the chill and let the flavours marry.

Meanwhile, make the creamy horseradish sauce. Mix together the sour cream, horseradish, cream, shallot and Dijon in a small bowl, and season with salt and pepper. Cover with clingfilm and refrigerate.

Preheat the oven to 200°C/gas mark 6.

Heat the remaining 2 tablespoons oil in a large ovenproof frying pan over a medium-high heat until it's shimmering but not smoking. Sear the beef so that it's browned on all sides – about 10 minutes in total. Add the 2 sprigs of rosemary to the pan and roast the beef in the oven for 15 minutes, or until a thermometer inserted into the thickest part of the meat reaches 52°C. Remove the roast to a chopping board and leave to rest for 20 minutes. Snip off the string and slice the beef into thin slices. Serve on a platter and pass the horseradish sauce around the table.

COOKING TIP

If you really want to take it easy, have your butcher tie the fillet up for you. It's all easy riding from there.

OVEN-ROASTED RIBS

Serves 4–6

Prep time: 15 minutes
Cook time: 1 hour 25 minutes

More often then not, I'll take advantage of our ten months of summer down here and cook my ribs out on the barbecue. But if you're stuck somewhere else that actually experiences winter, oven-roasted ribs are a great option. The best part about ribs is that you can crank up the rub and the sauce, giving it more or less heat, depending on your tolerance. Every region in the USA lays claim to certain varieties of BBQ sauce. North Carolina favours vinegar, Texas likes tomatoes and in Kansas City the sweeter and thicker, the better. I don't really have a dog in this fight; I like what tastes good and I've found that it's hard to beat this simple sauce, which brings together the best of every region's BBQ.

2 tablespoons soft light brown sugar

1 tablespoon mustard powder

1 tablespoon paprika

2 teaspoons smoked paprika

1 teaspoon freshly ground black pepper

1 teaspoon garlic salt

2 racks baby back pork ribs, 1.8kg in total

JAMIE'S TANGY BBQ SAUCE
(MAKES ABOUT 900G)

1 tablespoon rapeseed oil

$1/2$ small red onion, finely chopped

sea salt and freshly ground black pepper

360g tomato ketchup

240ml cider vinegar

160g soft light brown sugar

3 tablespoons Dijon mustard

1 tablespoon Worcestershire sauce

2 teaspoons chilli powder

$1/2$ teaspoon cayenne pepper

Preheat the oven to 180°C/gas mark 4. Line a baking tray with heavy-duty foil.

Mix together the brown sugar, mustard, paprika, smoked paprika, black pepper and garlic salt in a small bowl. Be sure to break up any lumps with your fingers. Reserve 1 tablespoon of the rub in a cup for serving.

Remove the silver skin from the underside of the ribs by sliding your fingers under the thin membrane and pulling it off. Repeat this step with the second rack. Rub the ribs with the seasoning mix on both sides. Place the ribs in a single layer on the prepared baking tray and cover tightly with heavy-duty foil. Bake for about 1 hour 15 minutes until the ribs are tender. (Be careful when removing the foil – there will be hot steam!)

Meanwhile, make the Tangy BBQ Sauce. Heat the oil in a medium saucepan over a medium-high heat. Add the onion and cook, stirring, for about 5 minutes until softened. Season with salt and pepper, then stir in the ketchup, vinegar, brown sugar, Dijon, Worcestershire sauce, chilli powder and cayenne pepper. Season again with some more salt and black pepper. Bring the sauce to the boil, then reduce to a simmer, set on medium-low heat, and cook until for about 35 minutes until the sauce is thickened.

Set your grill to medium heat. Adjust the shelf so that your ribs will be about 13cm from the heat source.

Grill one rack of ribs at a time for about 3 minutes until they are nice and brown. Remove them from the grill and brush on some sauce, and then grill again for about 3 minutes until the sauce is caramelised. Repeat with the second rack. (Grilling one rack at a time ensures that you can put each one directly under the grill.)

Leave the racks to rest for 5 minutes before slicing them into individual ribs. Sprinkle the cut ribs with the reserved dry rub and serve with extra sauce alongside.

HOBO DINNERS

Pretty much every kid thinks about running away from home at one time or another – and thank goodness most of 'em don't get past the front gate. I imagined following the railway tracks out of town, thinking that they'd lead me to something magical, or at least away from Albany. There's nothing wrong with my hometown – it still holds a real big place in my heart – but back when I was a kid, I felt the same about Albany as I did about my mom: both were a little embarrassing sometimes, but I couldn't deny that I belonged to them. One word out of my mouth and you knew exactly who and where I came from.

Sometimes Bobby and I would get real serious about moving on. We'd each put some ham sandwiches in a handkerchief, tie it around a long broom handle and sling it over our shoulders like we had seen Bugs Bunny do on the Saturday morning cartoons. We'd only get a couple of blocks down the street before we ate our sandwiches. Out of food, back home we'd come – just in time for supper.

When I gave up on the idea of living life on the lam, I joined the Boy Scouts of America for some adventure. As a Cub Scout, I loved everything about camping – the fire, ghost stories, sleeping under the stars – everything, that is, except for the food. For dinner we'd put hamburger, potatoes, carrots and onions in a packet of foil and cook it right there in the campfire. Because there was no temperature gauge, you had to kind of guess when you thought it was cooked through. It was a great idea, but the problem was it didn't actually taste good. It just tasted like fire.

I complained to mom about the 'hobo dinners' and she agreed that there was room for improvement. She refined the concept by bringing it indoors and adding some herbs – a foreign concept to the Boy Scouts at the time. I never forgot those foil-packet dinners Mom made and how well the flavours married together. I've included three recipes here that use chicken, fish and hamburger, and paired them with a seasonal vegetable. If they'd served meals like this back then, I might've made Eagle Scout.

FISH WITH COURGETTE AND BUTTER BEANS

Serves 4

Prep time: 10 minutes
Cook time: 20 minutes

I decided to try my hand at cooking fish in a foil packet because I didn't want the juices running all over the oven. More than that, I didn't want to get stuck cleaning it up. But I was actually surprised how good the fish tasted when its flavours married together with the vegetables and herbs in the packet, which you could change seasonally and get a different dish each time. And the after-dinner washing-up was a doddle; I literally tossed out the baking tray.

1 medium courgette, diced

1 x 400g can butter beans, rinsed and drained

150g baby plum tomatoes, sliced in half

3 garlic cloves, finely chopped

3 tablespoons olive oil

4 tablespoons torn fresh basil leaves

sea salt and freshly ground black pepper

4 skinless red snapper fillets, about 175g each

Preheat the oven to 200°C/gas mark 6.

Combine the courgette, butter beans, tomatoes, garlic, oil and basil in a medium mixing bowl. Season with salt and pepper and toss it all together. Divide the vegetables evenly between four squares of baking parchment placed on four squares of heavy-duty foil. Season the fish on both sides with salt and pepper and place one fillet on each square of foil. Make foil pouches by sealing all sides of the foil. Place the sealed packets on a baking tray and roast for 25 minutes until the fish is cooked through and the vegetables are soft.

CHICKEN WITH LEEKS AND SWEDE

Serves 4

Prep time: 10 minutes
Cook time: 45 minutes

I always have a lot to say about swedes (or rutabagas to us) because they're one of my favourite vegetables. They rarely get the praise they deserve, and often get confused with a turnip. Leeks are similar in that some people aren't sure what to do with 'em. Are they spring onions? They're actually not. Leeks are a not-too-distant cousin to spring onions and garlic, but at the end of the day, the sweet and mild taste of a leek puts it in a category all its own.

3 medium swedes, cut into 5mm-thick slices

2 medium leeks, rinsed, trimmed and sliced

2 teaspoons chopped fresh thyme

1 tablespoon chopped fresh rosemary

3 tablespoons olive oil

sea salt and freshly ground black pepper

4 boneless, skinless chicken breasts, 175g each

30g butter, sliced into $1/2$ tablespoon pats

Preheat the oven to 180°C/gas mark 4.

In a large bowl, combine the swede, leeks, thyme, rosemary and oil. Season with salt and pepper and toss it all together. Divide and layer the vegetables evenly between four squares of baking parchment placed on four squares of heavy-duty foil. Season the chicken breasts on both sides with salt and pepper and top each vegetable pile with a breast. Spoon any remaining herbs and leeks from the bowl on top of the chicken – you don't want to waste any flavour here. Top each breast with a pat of butter. Make foil pouches by sealing all sides of the foil. Place on a baking tray and roast for 45 minutes until the chicken is cooked through and the vegetables are soft.

HAMBURGER WITH CARROTS, POTATOES AND ONION

Serves 4

Prep time: 10 minutes
Cook time: 40 minutes

This is, quite literally, a meat-and-potatoes kind of recipe, one that I've finessed from my Cub Scout days. If you're looking to make something quick and hearty, this is the meal for you – and nearly every other hungry man on the planet.

675g lean beef mince

25g fresh breadcrumbs

50g Parmesan cheese, finely grated

1 medium egg, beaten

1 tablespoon Worcestershire sauce

3 garlic cloves, finely chopped

sea salt and freshly ground black pepper

1 medium sweet onion, thinly sliced

2 medium carrots, well scrubbed and sliced 5mm thick

4 medium Yukon gold or Maris Piper potatoes, well scrubbed and sliced 5mm thick

2 tablespoons olive oil

Preheat the oven to 180°C/gas mark 4. Mix together the beef, breadcrumbs, half of the Parmesan, egg, Worcestershire sauce and garlic in a large bowl. Season with a good pinch of salt and pepper. Form into four 15cm patties.

Add the carrots and potatoes to the bowl, drizzle with the oil and season with salt and pepper. Divide the vegetables evenly between four squares of baking parchment placed on four squares of heavy-duty foil. Top each with a hamburger patty and sprinkle the remaining Parmesan on top. Make foil pouches by sealing all sides of the foil. Place on a baking tray and roast for 40 minutes until the burger is cooked through and the vegetables are soft.

BY SEA

By Sea

Fish can be a hard sell to kids. They're slippery, sometimes smell funny and you can catch 'em off the end of a dock with a squiggly worm. Part of the problem is that there's little distance between the creature on the end of the hook and the fillet on the plate. We call meat from a pig 'pork', whereas fish is, well, just fish. In this case, a rose by any other name would mean that a lot more kids would be willing to eat fish.

It took me a long time to come around to eating fish and it wasn't from a lack of exposure. Lake Chehaw is a big beautiful lake, about ten miles wide, in the middle of Albany where Mom and Dad used to take us to catch freshwater fish for dinner. Other times we'd visit my Aunt Glynnis and Uncle Bernie's place in Statesboro, Georgia, which had this quiet pond where we'd fish and swat mosquitoes during long summer evenings. We'd have 'fish frys' with catfish, brim and crappie, but I never really liked it. Eventually, Bobby and I got smart and we'd catch the fish and release them real quick before Mom and Dad would know what had happened, guaranteeing us hot dogs for dinner.

My palate started to expand when we moved out here to the coast. I've tried more seafood than you can imagine and really started to enjoy certain kinds of fish. I discovered cuts of fish that are similar to steak in texture, like a satisfying salmon 'steak', but without any of the heaviness of red meat. And I learned the hard way that quality and freshness matter, but at least I've lived to tell about it.

Today I like fish, especially a flaky white halibut or flounder, just as much as I like steak – but like all meats, preparation is key. With fish, simple, fresh flavours are best – a squeeze of lemon here, a dollop of pesto there. It's good for you, it's easy to prepare and it cooks quickly. But you don't want to overcook fish because it'll dry out something awful.

What about prawns, you ask? Shrimp (prawns) is and always has been my seafood exception. As far as I'm concerned, they don't come from the sea but come down from Heaven, descending on a buttery cloud of grits.

BARBECUED SALMON ON WHITE WINE–SOAKED CEDAR PLANKS

Serves 4

Prep time: 5 minutes
Cook time: 25 minutes

After tearing apart half the North Atlantic fish population trying to find the perfect way to barbecue fish, I discovered cooking with cedar planks, which sounds more complicated than it is. I just soak the planks in any white wine that I have on hand and source my seasonings from about 6 metres away, plucking lemons from my tree in the garden and cutting a few sprigs of rosemary from a nearby bush. Fresh homegrown seasonings and a wine-soaked cedar plank? Sounds like a 28-dollar dinner to me.

2 cedar planks, 30cm x 15cm

1 bottle dry white wine

2 skinless salmon fillets, 450g each

sea salt and freshly ground black pepper

extra-virgin olive oil

8 lemon slices

6 sprigs of fresh rosemary

Soak the cedar planks in the white wine in a large baking tin for 2 hours.

Heat a gas barbecue with the lid closed on a high heat for 15 minutes. Once it's preheated, place the cedar planks directly on the hot barbecue rack and cook for 1 minute on each side.

Prepare for indirect barbecuing. Turn off the burner on one side of the barbecue, and adjust the heat on the other side to medium-high. Season the salmon on both sides with salt and pepper, then place both fillets, skin side down, on the planks. Drizzle the salmon lightly with olive oil and top with the lemon and rosemary. Move the cedar planks to the side of the barbecue with no heat. Close the lid and cook for 20–25 minutes, with the lid closed, until the salmon is opaque and cooked through.

COOKING TIP

The typical cedar planks you see for sale fit a 450g piece of fish nicely. So, for a good-looking presentation, I use two planks.

It's important to soak the planks because otherwise they'll on catch fire. It's wood, y'all.

ROASTED PESTO SALMON WITH BABY PLUM TOMATOES

Serves 4

Prep time: 5 minutes
Cook time: 30 minutes

Bobby is a huge fish eater and Brooke likes salmon a lot. I wasn't the biggest fan of creatures of the finned variety, but this recipe changed my tune. I dressed up salmon fillets with two things I really love – roasted tomatoes and pesto. It's just as easy as covering the salmon in butter and lemon, but it tastes like you really killed yourself in the kitchen. If you only 'kind of' like salmon, try this dish and you'll *really* like salmon – it worked for me.

550g baby plum tomatoes

1 tablespoon olive oil

sea salt and freshly ground black pepper

4 skinless salmon fillets, 175g each

120g Basil Pesto (recipe below)

dried chilli flakes (optional)

BASIL PESTO
(MAKES ABOUT 300G)

115g fresh basil leaves

120ml extra-virgin olive oil

35g Parmesan cheese, finely grated

35g pine nuts, toasted and cooled

2 large garlic cloves, peeled

sea salt and freshly ground black pepper

Preheat the oven to 200°C/gas mark 6. Line a baking tray with foil.

Arrange the tomatoes on the baking tray, drizzle with the oil and season well with salt and pepper. Roast for 10 minutes.

Meanwhile, make your basil pesto. Add the basil, oil, Parmesan, pine nuts and garlic to the bowl of a food processor and pulse until the mixture is smooth. Taste for seasoning, adding some salt and pepper.

Season both sides of the salmon fillets with salt and pepper. Top each fillet with a generous 2-tablespoon dollop of fresh pesto and spread it across the top. (Reserve the remaining pesto for another use.)

Remove the tomatoes from the oven and add the salmon to the baking tray. Roast for a further 10 minutes until the tomatoes are soft and the salmon is cooked through. Give the tomatoes one more pinch of salt.

Serve the salmon topped with the roasted tomatoes. Adults can sprinkle the tomatoes with a hit of chilli flakes for some kick, if they like.

 COOKING TIP

Serve this with a side of rice or couscous for an easy weeknight meal. I make my homemade pesto by blending Parmesan, pine nuts and the basil we get from our herb garden in the summer. The sauce can last up to six months in the freezer, which means you can enjoy this otherwise seasonal dish year round.

OVEN-ROASTED GARLICKY PRAWNS

Serves 4

Prep time: 5 minutes
Cook time: 10 minutes

Living in Savannah, Georgia, there's so many prawns (shrimp) to be had that we've found a million different ways to prepare it. This is a good way that's really simple and you can do it with any type of prawn. It's no fuss – you just pop it in the oven. If only getting the kids to bed were this easy . . .

675g raw large king or tiger prawns, peeled and deveined

3 tablespoons olive oil

2 garlic cloves, roughly chopped

1 teaspoon roughly chopped fresh rosemary

sea salt and freshly ground black pepper

Preheat the oven to 200°C/gas mark 6.

Toss together the prawns, oil, garlic and rosemary on a baking tray and season with salt and pepper. Roast for 10 minutes, or just until the prawns are opaque and cooked through (they can get chewy quickly).

Transfer the prawns to a bowl, then pour any remaining garlic and oil from the baking tray over the prawns. You can eat as is or serve over rice or a big salad for dinner.

What's ratatouille? Pretty much, it's just a fun way to describe sautéed vegetables. Some chefs can get kind of particular about what defines the traditional dish, but without overthinking it, it's basically a vegetable hash that includes tomatoes, peppers, aubergine, courgette and basil. The addition of a mild and affordable fish such as halibut upgrades ratatouille from a side dish to a main one.

PAN-ROASTED HALIBUT WITH RATATOUILLE

Serves 4

Prep time: 25 minutes
Cook time: 45 minutes

To make the ratatouille, preheat the oven to 200°C/gas mark 6.

Place your tomatoes on a baking tray, drizzle with 1 tablespoon oil and season with salt and pepper. Toss it all together and roast for 15 minutes.

To make the ratatouille, heat the remaining 3 tablespoons oil in a large flameproof casserole dish over a medium-high heat. Once it's hot, add the onion, garlic and pepper and sauté for about 5 minutes until they're tender. Season with a big hit of salt and pepper. Stir in the tomato purée and cook for 1 minute, continually stirring, toasting it to really develop the flavour. Add the aubergine and courgette next, and sauté for about another 6 minutes until the aubergine is completely tender. Add the roasted tomatoes and their juices and the stock and simmer for a further 25–30 minutes until everything is all nice and stew-like. Taste again for seasoning and adjust the salt and pepper as needed. Stir in the basil, butter and chilli flakes (or skip the chilli if it's too much heat for your kids). Cover to keep warm.

Meanwhile, heat the oil in a large non-stick frying pan until it shimmers. Pat the fish dry with kitchen paper and season it on both sides with salt and pepper. Add the halibut to the hot oil and cook over a medium heat for about 5 minutes until nicely browned on the bottom. Flip the fish to the other side and cook for about 3 minutes longer.

Garnish with some fresh basil and serve the ratatouille on the side.

RATATOUILLE

600g cherry tomatoes

4 tablespoons olive oil

sea salt and freshly ground black pepper

1 medium red onion, finely chopped

4 garlic cloves, roughly chopped

1 red pepper, chopped

1 tablespoon tomato purée

1 medium aubergine (675g), peeled and cut into 2.5cm cubes

1 medium courgette, chopped

240ml Homemade Chicken Stock (page 205)

4 tablespoons torn fresh basil leaves

30g butter

$1/8$ teaspoon dried chilli flakes (optional)

2 tablespoons olive oil

4 pieces skinless halibut, 175g each

sea salt and freshly ground black pepper

fresh basil leaves for serving

FROGMORE STEW

Serves 4, generously

Prep time: 10 minutes
Cook time: 40 minutes

A Lowcountry Boil is reason alone for Southerners to gather and celebrate. Its less familiar cousin, Frogmore Stew, is in the same family but carries the traditional name. Frogmore was actually a small fishing community located just outside of Beaufort, South Carolina – a short day trip from Savannah, Georgia. While the town no longer exists, the legend of where the historic recipe originated endures. It's a very communal meal. All of the ingredients go into one big pot, and when it's done cooking, you can just dump it out on some newspaper and stand around the table and eat it. It's not fancy, but there's nothing like it.

2 tablespoons olive oil

450g smoked cooked pork sausage or kielbasa, cut on the bias into 2.5cm pieces

1 medium sweet onion, chopped

2 celery sticks with leaves, chopped

sea salt and freshly ground black pepper

4 tablespoons seafood seasoning (such as Old Bay), plus more for serving

350ml beer

1 tablespoon soft light brown sugar

2.4 litres water

1 bay leaf

1 head garlic, sliced in half

1 lemon, quartered

45g butter

450g small new potatoes

3 corn on the cob, husked and cut crossways into 3 or 4 pieces

675g raw shell-on large king or tiger prawns

warm bread for serving

hot sauce for serving

Heat the olive oil in a large saucepan over a medium-high heat. Once it's hot, add the sausage pieces and cook, while stirring, for 4–5 minutes until they're nice and browned on all sides. Transfer the sausage to a bowl and set aside.

Add the onion and celery to the pan and sauté for about 5 minutes until soft. Season the mixture with a big pinch of salt and pepper, then sprinkle in the seafood seasoning and toast, while stirring, for 1 minute. Pour in the beer and scrape up any browned bits that may have stuck to the bottom of the pan. Cook the beer down for 5 minutes; it should reduce by half. Stir in the brown sugar.

Add the water, bay leaf, garlic, lemon, butter, potatoes and corn. Bring the water up to a simmer, then cover and cook for about 17 minutes until the potatoes are cooked through.

Add the prawns and reserved sausage, bring the stew back up to a simmer and cook for a further 5 minutes.

Pour the stew out on a newspaper-lined table. Serve with warm bread, your favourite hot sauce, some Old Bay and lots of beer.

INGREDIENT NOTE

We add four live blue crabs to the pot after the potatoes have cooked for about 10 minutes or halfway through, but you could add small live spider crabs, langoustine or crayfish instead if available, or feel free to add what comes to hand.

I've never seen picky eaters turn their noses up at Frogmore Stew; there's something in it for everybody.

'Shrimp 'n' grits' was traditionally a poor man's breakfast for shrimpers in the South Carolina Lowcountry. Today, the dish has had a high-class makeover and can be found on five-star menus all over the country. But to me, the best shrimp 'n' grits are still cooked up in the Southeastern kitchens where they originated. I make mine with fresh wild Georgia shrimp (prawns) that taste like they were pulled from the net minutes before I brought them home. I've prepared shrimp 'n' grits with barbecued shrimp and a brown sauce, but here we're doing a rich cream sauce that really speaks to our area. It's one of my favourite lunches to cook for Brooke – when we have time to indulge.

CLASSIC SAVANNAH 'SHRIMP 'N' GRITS'

Serves 4

Prep time: 15 minutes
Cook time: 25 minutes

Add the water to a heavy-based saucepan over a medium-high heat and season it with salt and pepper. Bring to a simmer, reduce the heat to medium and pour in the grits in a slow, steady stream while whisking. Cook the grits, stirring occasionally, for about 30 minutes until they're thick and creamy. Stir in the cream, Parmesan and butter. Taste your grits for seasoning and adjust as necessary. Cover to keep warm.

Season the prawns with salt and pepper. Heat the butter and oil in a large sauté pan over a medium-high heat until melted and foamy. Add the sausage and onion and sauté for 5–6 minutes until the onion is tender and the sausage is browned. Add the prawns and cook for just 1 minute on each side. Once the prawns are opaque, remove them with a slotted spoon to a plate and reserve. Add the tomatoes to the pan along with a big pinch of salt and pepper, and cook, stirring, for a further 3–4 minutes until they have softened and broken down. Stir in the wine and reduce for about 3 minutes until the mixture is almost dry. Stir in the cream and then reduce for about a further 5 minutes until the sauce can coat the back of a spoon. Return the prawns to the pan and cook for another minute.

Divide the grits between four bowls and top with a heap of prawns and sauce. Garnish with some spring onions and serve with hot sauce – or don't, if you can't take the heat.

COOKING TIP

Cook quick-cooking grits like regular grits – low and slow – so that they come out extra creamy.

GRITS

950ml water

sea salt and freshly ground black pepper

150g quick-cooking grits

120ml double cream

2 tablespoons freshly grated Parmesan cheese

30g butter

SHRIMP

450g raw large king or tiger prawns, peeled and deveined

sea salt and freshly ground black pepper

15g butter

1 tablespoon olive oil

175g smoked cooked pork sausage or kielbasa, finely chopped

1/2 sweet onion, finely diced

1 small green pepper, finely diced

2 medium plum tomatoes, deseeded and diced

120ml dry white wine

120ml double cream

sliced spring onions for serving

hot sauce for serving (optional)

It used to be that only poor folks ate 'shrimp 'n' grits'. Now this dish can run you 28 dollars (17 pounds) in New york City at lunchtime.

DRY-BOILED LEMON PRAWNS

Serves 6

Prep time: 10 minutes
Cook time: 15 minutes

Donna Foltz, one of Momma's good friends, hosts a Christmas party every year and asks her guests to bring a dish. And every year, sometime in June, she reminds me to bring my potato salad, which is her favourite. But it's her Dry-boiled Lemon Prawns that everyone scrambles to get. I hadn't heard of 'dry-boiling' until she showed me the technique; she cooks her prawns in just a little bit of liquid with a whole lot of seafood and Cajun seasoning.

900g raw shell-on large king or tiger prawns

2 tablespoons seafood seasoning (preferably Zatarain's Crawfish, Shrimp & Crab Boil in a Bag)

$1/2$ teaspoon Cajun seasoning

1 teaspoon sea salt

1 tablespoon cider vinegar

1 small onion, roughly chopped

1 celery stick, roughly chopped

1 bay leaf

4 sprigs of fresh thyme

2 garlic cloves, smashed

55g butter, sliced into pats

1 lemon, halved

Combine the prawns, seafood and Cajun seasonings, salt, vinegar, onion, celery, bay leaf, thyme and garlic cloves in a large, heavy-based saucepan. Top with the butter slices, squeeze in the lemon juice and toss the lemon shells into the pot as well. Cover with a lid, turn the heat to medium and cook for 12 minutes, removing the lid and stirring every few minutes. Turn off the heat and let the prawns rest for just 3 minutes before serving.

OVEN-FRIED HADDOCK FILLETS

Serves 4

Prep time: 10 minutes
Cook time: 20 minutes

Jack's and Matthew's love of fish is one reason we don't fry in our house. Here, 'oven-fried' is code for 'baked'. Without all that fat and oil, I create that same crunchiness by dredging the fillets in panko. The result is a lighter coating that maintains its crispy texture when baked – and I don't have to feel bad when they ask for another 'fish stick'.

4 large haddock (or cod or halibut) fillets, 175–225g each

sea salt and freshly ground black pepper

95g plain flour

120ml full-fat milk

2 egg whites

2 teaspoons Dijon mustard

150g panko breadcrumbs

$1/8$ teaspoon cayenne pepper

1 tablespoon finely chopped fresh parsley

45g butter, melted

lemons, cut into wedges, for serving

Preheat the oven to 220°C/gas mark 7 with a shelf in the middle. Line a baking tray with foil and coat with non-stick cooking spray.

Pat the fish dry with kitchen paper and season each side with salt and pepper. Place three baking dishes in front of you. Add the flour to the first; the milk, egg whites and Dijon to the second (whisking well to combine); and the panko, cayenne, parsley and butter to the third (tossing all together really well). Dredge each fillet first through the flour, then the egg and finally the panko. Arrange on the baking tray.

Bake for 15–17 minutes until the fillets are just lightly golden and flake easily when poked with a fork. To finish, grill for 1–2 minutes until golden brown.

OODLES AND OODLES

Oodles and Oodles

Other than spaghetti or 'mac 'n' cheese' (macaroni cheese to you), we didn't have a lot of pasta growing up. Thank goodness, otherwise we'd be big as barn doors. I started to eat more pasta when Jack moved to table food because he liked it so much, but I didn't want a carb overload. Instead, I incorporated as many vegetables and proteins as I could into each dish, playing around with different recipes that would provide a well-balanced meal the whole family could enjoy.

Watching Mario Batali cook has really turned me on to Italian and he's been a huge influence in how I approach pasta. He's such a nice guy and a talented chef who knows his way around linguine better than anyone. In the process, I've become smarter about different ways to quickly throw together pasta dishes that are so much more than just noodles and sauce. These days I really enjoy eating pasta, which is good because now that Matthew has come to the table, we're eating pasta more than ever.

I approach pasta as the foundation for a dish. To that I add whatever seasonal vegetables I have on hand, a tasty sauce and sometimes a protein. Some of my favourite recipes have come about this way, including Autumn Lasagne with Sage and Squash Purée.

Every pasta recipe in this chapter can be modified to meet your needs, whether you want fewer vegetables or more protein. The real beauty of these pasta recipes is that you can turn pretty much anything in your fridge – including last night's roast chicken – into something new and more exciting than leftovers. It's a quick choose-your-own-adventure way of eating that keeps dinnertime interesting – and your refrigerator from overflowing.

THREE-CHEESE STUFFED SHELLS WITH SPINACH AND ZESTY TURKEY TOMATO SAUCE

Serves 10 (5 servings per baking dish)

Prep time: 30 minutes
Cook time: 1 hour

It goes without saying that with kids in the family, we're gonna eat a lot of pasta and cheese. But there is a limit to how much 'mac 'n' cheese' a man can eat – even a Southern one. In this recipe I take what the boys like and present it in something other than the shape of an elbow. Jack loves helping me stuff the shells. The only problem is teaching Matthew that not all shells are fit for eating when we hit the beach.

350g jumbo pasta shells (conchiglioni rigati)

1 tablespoon olive oil

450g turkey sausages, casings removed

1 small onion, finely chopped

sea salt and freshly ground black pepper

2 garlic cloves, finely chopped

$1/4$ teaspoon dried chilli flakes

2 x 350g cans passata rustica (crushed tomatoes) or 2 x 400g cans finely chopped Italian tomatoes

400g can tomato purée

$3/4$ teaspoon Italian seasoning

425g ricotta cheese

280g frozen spinach, defrosted and squeezed of excess water

25g Parmesan cheese, finely grated

2 medium eggs, lightly beaten

225g grated firm mozzarella cheese or half-fat fresh mozzarella, diced

Bring a large saucepan of salted water to the boil. Cook the pasta shells for 1 minute less than it says on the packet. Drain and leave to cool.

Preheat the oven to 180°C/gas mark 4. Spray two 23cm x 33cm baking dishes with non-stick cooking spray.

Heat a large, high-sided frying pan over a medium-high heat. Add the oil and, once it's hot, add the sausage meat and cook for 3–4 minutes until browned, stirring and breaking it up with the back of a wooden spoon. Stir in the onion and cook for about 4 minutes until softened. Season the mixture with a big pinch of salt and pepper, then stir in the garlic and chilli flakes and cook for 1 minute until fragrant. Stir in the passata or chopped tomatoes, tomato purée, Italian seasoning and 120ml water and simmer it all over a medium-low heat, uncovered, for 15 minutes. Give it a taste for seasoning and add a big pinch of salt if needed.

Meanwhile, add the ricotta, spinach, Parmesan, eggs and half of the mozzarella to a large bowl, season with salt and pepper and give it a stir until well combined.

Spread three ladlefuls of sauce on the bottom of each prepared baking dish. Stuff each shell with 1 heaped tablespoon of cheese mixture. Place 20 stuffed shells in each dish, then cover with even more sauce. Sprinkle each with half of the mozzarella. Cover with foil and bake for 35 minutes, removing the foil for the last 5 minutes of baking.

If you want to freeze the second dish, make sure it has cooled completely; cover with clingfilm, then a layer of foil, and freeze for up to 3 months. Defrost completely in the refrigerator; bake as directed above.

INGREDIENT NOTE

If you're not a fan of turkey sausages, feel free to sub in pork sausages.

COOKING TIP

This recipe makes a double batch, which is great to do when making almost any baked pasta dish since they freeze and reheat so well.

QUICK LEMON AND BASIL LINGUINE

Serves 4–6

Prep time: 5 minutes
Cook time: 20 minutes

This is a very simple recipe that's both comforting and delicious, making it perfect for a weekday dinner.

Forget packets of seasoning and powdery orange cheese – quick and affordable cooking doesn't have to mean compromising taste and quality. This one-pot meal literally takes just minutes to prepare, but the addition of fresh lemon zest and strips of basil make it a home run. Move into the next tax bracket by adding chicken or prawns.

450g linguine

4 tablespoons extra-virgin olive oil

2 garlic cloves, thinly sliced

60ml double cream

juice from 1 large lemon (about 60ml)

sea salt and freshly ground black pepper

50g Parmesan cheese, freshly grated, plus more for serving

2 teaspoons finely grated lemon zest

20g fresh basil, thinly sliced, plus more for serving

Cook the pasta in a large saucepan of boiling salted water until al dente. Reserve 120ml of the pasta water, then drain your pasta in a colander.

Heat the oil in the same pan you cooked your pasta in. Once it's hot, add the garlic and cook, stirring, for about 2 minutes until the edges just begin to turn golden brown. Stir in the cream and lemon juice, and season with a pinch of salt and pepper. Simmer for 2 minutes, then toss in the Parmesan, lemon zest and, finally, the cooked pasta.

Bring the heat to medium and, with tongs, thoroughly toss the pasta through the sauce while drizzling in the reserved pasta water, just to loosen up the sauce a bit. Season with freshly ground black pepper and turn off the heat. Toss the pasta with the basil just before serving. Serve in bowls, sprinkled with some extra Parmesan and torn basil.

COOKING TIP

I like to pick my battles when it comes to getting my kids to eat. While this recipe calls for linguine, if pasta 'tunnels' or 'wheels' float your kid's boat, then by all means go with that.

We don't actually have any vegetarians in our family. Not any that we've accepted, anyway.

Lasagne is a dish that I recommend for those of you who are just starting off in the kitchen. It's relatively easy (or pretty hard to screw up, depending on how you want to look at it). Here, we're going homemade with our own creamy béchamel sauce, which is a fancy French way of saying 'white sauce'. With the addition of seasonal butternut squash and sage, both fresh from our garden, this makes for a big, warm, comforting dish that's a little unexpected. It's so good, even the staunchest carnivores won't notice it's vegetarian; or if they do, they won't care.

AUTUMN LASAGNE WITH SAGE AND SQUASH PUREE

Serves 8

Prep time: 20 minutes
Cook time: 1 hour 30 minutes

Preheat the oven to 200°C/gas mark 6. Line a baking tray with foil. Place the squash on the tray and drizzle with the oil. Toss well and season with salt and pepper. Roast for about 30 minutes until soft. Transfer to a food processor with the stock, season again and blend until smooth.

Grease a 23 x 33cm baking dish with butter. Reduce the oven temperature to 190°C/gas mark 5.

Melt 115g of the butter in a large saucepan over a medium heat. Twist and bruise the sage leaves to release their flavour and cook, stirring and flipping and bruising the leaves with a wooden spoon, until they are crisp but the butter is not yet brown. Using a slotted spoon, transfer the sage leaves to a plate and set aside. Sprinkle the flour into the saucepan and stir over a medium heat for about 2 minutes until pasty. Slowly pour in the milk, whisking constantly. Return the sage to the milk and whisk as the mixture comes to the boil. Reduce to a simmer and cook for 15 minutes, stirring every few minutes to keep the sauce from burning onto the bottom of the pan. Season well with salt, pepper and a dash of nutmeg.

Ladle a thin layer of the sage cream sauce on the bottom of the buttered dish. Lay four lasagne sheets in the pan, overlapping slightly. Add another ladleful of the sauce to cover the pasta, top with one-fourth of the squash purée, then sprinkle with one-fourth of the mozzarella and Parmesan. Repeat the layering two more times, then ladle on the remaining white sauce and dollop the lasagne with the squash purée. Sprinkle with the remaining mozzarella and Parmesan and garnish with a few sage leaves. Dot the remaining 30g butter on the top. Cover the lasagne tightly with foil and bake for 40 minutes. Remove the foil and bake for a further 20 minutes until golden and bubbling.

1 butternut squash, about 1.3kg, peeled, deseeded and cut into 2.5cm cubes

2 tablespoons olive oil

sea salt and freshly ground black pepper

350ml low-salt or Homemade Chicken Stock (page 205)

145g butter, cut into 15g pats, plus more for greasing

8 fresh sage leaves, plus more for serving

65g plain flour

1.1 litres full-fat milk

dash of freshly grated nutmeg

250g no-precook lasagne sheets (I like the Barilla brand)

170g grated firm mozzarella cheese or half-fat fresh mozzarella, diced

50g Parmesan cheese, finely grated

SPAGHETTI WITH TURKEY MEATBALLS

Serves 4–6

Prep time: 30 minutes
Cook time: 40 minutes

When I was younger, the first dish I ever made to impress a girl was baked spaghetti. I'm not sure what she tired of first – my obsession with comic books or my carbo-loading – but let's just say my love affair with spaghetti far outlasted our love affair. As they say in the South, 'Bless her heart'. Because this dish is so easy and kids love it, every family has to have it in their weekly rotation. If you're short on time, you can exchange my basic tomato sauce with a shop-bought variety. I cut back on fat by using turkey in the meatballs instead of red meat, and baking rather than frying them. My children haven't noticed these small changes. My belt loops have.

1 medium egg, lightly beaten

60ml full-fat milk

1/2 small onion, finely chopped

2 garlic cloves, very finely chopped

45g panko breadcrumbs

50g Parmesan cheese, finely grated, plus more for serving

15g finely chopped fresh flat-leaf parsley

550g turkey thigh mince

1 tablespoon olive oil

1kg Basic Tomato Sauce (page 206)

450g spaghetti (or your favourite pasta)

Preheat the oven to 200°C/gas mark 6. Lightly oil a baking tray.

Combine the egg, milk, onion, garlic, breadcrumbs, Parmesan and parsley in a large bowl. Fold in the turkey and gently mix all together. Form into 4cm golf ball-sized meatballs. Place them on the prepared baking tray, drizzle lightly with olive oil and bake for 20–25 minutes, or until the meatballs are lightly golden and cooked through.

Put the tomato sauce in a large, high-sided frying pan or saucepan and bring to a simmer. Add the meatballs and simmer for 10 minutes.

Cook your favourite pasta according to the packet instructions. Add your pasta to the saucepan with the tomato sauce and meatballs and gently toss it all together.

Serve the spaghetti and meatballs in bowls with some extra Parmesan sprinkled on top.

INGREDIENT NOTE

The dark meat is where you're going to get a lot of the flavour, so look for turkey thigh mince in preference to turkey breast mince.

COOKING TIPS

Making your own meatballs is super-easy – just be sure you have a cover for your pan or it's gonna look like your toddler finger-painted the kitchen with tomato sauce.

Meatballs are a great dish to double up on. Allow the extra meatballs to cool completely after baking, then place them in a single layer on a baking tray and pop them into the freezer. Once frozen, put 'em in a freezer bag and freeze for up to 3 months. Defrost in the fridge and reheat in a pot of simmering sauce.

CAULIFLOWER 'MAC 'N' CHEESE'

Serves 8

Prep Time: 10 minutes
Cook Time: 45 minutes

Get ready to work some magic. While sneaking cauliflower into traditional macaroni cheese doesn't exactly make it low-fat – we're still using full-fat milk and cheese – it's a great way to cut back on calorie-heavy pasta and throw in some added nutrition. How does it work? The cauliflower absorbs the creamy sauce, disguising the fact that half of this dish is actually vegetable and not pasta. And if you really don't want to show your hand to your friends and family, keep the recipe's name on the down-low.

Preheat the oven to 180°C/gas mark 4. Spray a 23cm x 33cm baking dish with non-stick cooking spray.

Bring a large saucepan of salted water to the boil. Add the pasta and set your timer for 4 minutes less than the time indicated on the back of the packet. Add the cauliflower once the timer sounds and cook for a further 4 minutes. Be sure the cauliflower is soft and the pasta is cooked through before draining.

Melt the butter in a large saucepan over a medium-high heat. Once it's foamy and melted, add the onion and garlic and cook for about 3 minutes until the onions are softened. Season with salt and pepper, then sprinkle in the flour and cook, while stirring, for a further 1 minute. Slowly whisk in the milk and bring it to a simmer; the sauce should begin to thicken at this point. Simmer, while stirring, for 5 minutes until the sauce is thick enough to coat the back of a spoon. Then knock the heat down to low and stir in 230g of the Cheddar, one handful at a time. Turn off the heat, stir in the sour cream, Dijon, hot sauce and cayenne and season the sauce to taste with salt and pepper. Stir in the pasta and cauliflower, making sure both are nice and coated with the sauce.

Pour the pasta and cauliflower mixture into the prepared baking dish. Sprinkle the top with the panko and the remaining Cheddar.

Bake for 35 minutes until the top is golden brown and bubbling. Let the mac cool and settle for 5 minutes before digging in.

INGREDIENT NOTE

If you want to lighten this up even more, use semi-skimmed milk instead of full-fat, half-fat mozzarella in place of the Cheddar and substitute half-fat sour cream for the full-fat version.

225g medium pasta shells

1 medium head cauliflower (800g), cored, cut into small florets and then roughly chopped

30g butter

1/2 small onion, finely chopped

2 garlic cloves, chopped

sea salt and freshly ground black pepper

2 tablespoons plain flour

600ml full-fat milk

280g extra-mature Cheddar cheese

80ml sour cream

1 teaspoon Dijon mustard

1 teaspoon hot sauce

1/8 teaspoon cayenne pepper

85g panko breadcrumbs

How do you turn something good into something awesome? Wrap it in bacon. This dish will blow you away because you begin with something that's hard to improve upon – plump, extra-large prawns, which really work well in this recipe because their size stands up to the strong bacon taste. The trick to this recipe is to bake the bacon halfway before wrapping it around the prawns, creating a crisp coating for the tender bite tucked inside. The bright freshness of the basil penne pasta pairs perfectly with the rich and savoury flavour of the bacon-prawn bites.

BACON-WRAPPED PRAWNS WITH BASIL PENNE PASTA

Serves 4–6

Prep time: 20 minutes
Cook time: 20 minutes

Preheat the oven to 200°C/gas mark 6. Line your baking tray with foil.

Arrange the bacon on the baking tray and bake for about 10 minutes until it's halfway done and not yet crisp. Remove the bacon to a kitchen paper-lined tray to drain and cool completely. Drain off and discard all but 1 tablespoon of fat in the pan (you can eyeball this). Once the bacon is cool, wrap each prawn with a half slice of bacon and line them up, seam side down, on the greased baking tray. Bake for 10 minutes until the bacon is crisp and the prawns are opaque and cooked through.

Add the pasta to a large saucepan of salted boiling water and cook for the time indicated on the packet. Reserve 60ml of the liquid used to cook the pasta.

Heat the oil in a large frying pan over a medium-high heat. Add the garlic and tomatoes, give them a stir and cook for 4–5 minutes until the tomatoes start to soften and melt down. Season the tomatoes with a big pinch of salt and pepper. Add the wine and cook, while stirring, for a further 3–4 minutes until the sauce has begun to thicken. Add the drained pasta to the pan, along with the reserved pasta cooking liquid, and toss everything together. Adjust your seasoning by adding a little more salt and pepper. Toss in the basil and gently fold in the bacon-wrapped prawns.

Divide the pasta equally between serving bowls and sprinkle with some Parmesan and chilli flakes, if desired.

8 smoked streaky bacon rashers, cut in half crossways

450g raw extra-large tiger or king prawns, peeled and deveined

450g penne pasta

4 tablespoons olive oil

4 garlic cloves, roughly chopped

450g baby plum tomatoes, sliced in half

sea salt and freshly ground black pepper

120ml dry white wine

4 tablespoons torn fresh basil leaves

Parmesan cheese for serving (optional)

dried chilli flakes for serving (optional)

BAKED AUBERGINE RIGATONI WITH FOUR CHEESES

Serves 8

Prep time: 20 minutes
Cook time: 1 hour 10 minutes

Beware of the sponge-like potential of aubergine. If you fry it as opposed to baking it, the aubergine soaks up every bit of oil you add, so you'll just keep adding more and more and more . . .

It took me some time to get up the nerve to cook with aubergine because I just couldn't wrap my head around the notion that it's a passable substitute for meat in any recipe. However, it does in fact add a satisfying meaty quality without all the excess oil and fat. I'm not about to become a full-fledged vegetarian over it, but I can testify that this aubergine and pasta dish is a tasty option.

1 small aubergine (550g), peeled and cut into 2.5cm cubes

4 tablespoons olive oil

sea salt and freshly ground black pepper

750g Basic Tomato Sauce (page 206)

2 tablespoons torn fresh basil

450g rigatoni pasta

225g half-fat mozzarella cheese, diced

250g ricotta cheese

80g fontina cheese, grated

25g Parmesan cheese, finely grated

Preheat the oven to 200°C/gas mark 6. Spray a 23cm x 33cm baking dish with non-stick cooking spray.

Place the aubergine on a baking tray, drizzle with the oil and season with salt and pepper. Toss well to combine. Roast the aubergine for 30–35 minutes until golden.

Transfer the aubergine to a large saucepan, cover with the tomato sauce and stir in the basil. Bring the whole thing up to a simmer and cook for 5 minutes to blend all the flavours together. Taste for seasoning and adjust accordingly.

Drop the oven temperature down to 180°C/gas mark 4.

Cook the pasta in boiling salted water according to packet instructions. Drain well, reserving 60ml of the pasta cooking liquid from the pan.

Add the pasta to the aubergine sauce and stir to combine, adding the pasta cooking liquid to loosen up the sauce only if needed. Transfer the aubergine pasta to the prepared baking dish. Stir in the mozzarella and dollop with the ricotta, giving it a gentle stir but not mixing the ricotta completely into the sauce. Top the whole thing off with the fontina and Parmesan. Bake for 35 minutes until bubbly and golden on top.

PICK A SIDE

Pick a Side

When it comes to side dishes, anything goes. From something as simple as a single gherkin to the more complex baked Wild Rice and Swiss Chard Gratin (page 142), a side dish really rounds out a meal. That's not to say that all sides are created equal. Anyone who's ever been served lasagne with a side of 'mac 'n' cheese' knows what I mean; it's all about successful pairing – choosing the right flavours, textures and even colours to complement the main dish. As good as a green bean casserole may be, pair it with braised spring greens and a warm spinach salad and you risk turning green just looking at your plate.

When invited to a dinner party, guests are often asked to bring a side, so it's good to have some go-to recipes in your arsenal. Some people even become known for their well-loved side dishes. My mom, for instance, is always asked to bring her 'mac 'n' cheese'. Brooke brings her popular strawberry pretzel salad that I refer to as Yes, a Jelly Salad (the jury is still out on whether this is a salad or a dessert, see page 172). The recipes in this chapter are some of the sides that have been requested of me time and time again by my family and friends alike. I've also included some tips about which foods these dishes pair well with to help you make a good match (Mexican rice with lasagne, for instance, is not a great combination).

The recipes in this chapter complement just about any main dish, travel well and pretty much guarantee you'll get an invite back – if you want it. If not, bring a bag of crisps. Half eaten.

SHAVED BRUSSELS SPROUTS WITH BACON AND PECANS

Serves 4–6

Prep time: 10 minutes
Cook time: 15 minutes

It's no wonder this dish is so good. You could put bacon and brown sugar on a paper plate and it'd be delicious.

You probably wouldn't ever put a Brussels sprout and a bikini model together, but it happens to be a pretty fantastic pairing. My mom called me one day and said, 'I've got a *Sports Illustrated* swimsuit model on the show today; would you like to be on the show, too?' Well, a son's gotta do what a son's gotta do. So I said to my wife, 'Momma told me I have to be on her show today.' It was really nice to meet this swimsuit model, but honestly, my favourite part of that day was when said model showed me how to make Brussels sprouts so they taste good. Cabbage is one of my favourite vegetables, so I thought that I would love Brussels sprouts because they're pretty much tiny cabbages. But they're *really* bitter. The trick to getting rid of that bitterness – and pretty much the secret to making any great dish – is that you've got to add a little bit of bacon and a little bit of sugar. This recipe here is a winner – a top model, dare I say.

675g Brussels sprouts, ends trimmed

2 thick-cut smoked streaky bacon rashers, sliced into 5mm strips

1/2 medium red onion, finely chopped

60g pecan nuts, roughly chopped

2 tablespoons cider vinegar

1 tablespoon soft light brown sugar

sea salt and freshly ground black pepper

Cut the Brussels sprouts in half, put them face down and thinly slice into ribbons. If this is just too tedious for you, an easier way to prep them is to slice them in a food processor fitted with a thin slicing disc.

Add the bacon to a large frying pan over a medium heat and slowly render out its fat. Continue cooking until the bacon is nice and crisp – 3–4 minutes in total. Using a slotted spoon, transfer the bacon to a kitchen paper-lined plate and set it aside just for the time being.

Turn the heat up to medium-high, add the onion and sauté for about 3 minutes until it's softened. Stir in the Brussels sprouts and sauté for about 5 minutes until they're tender-crisp. Stir in the pecans and cook, while stirring, for a further minute, then stir in the vinegar and brown sugar and season it all to taste with salt and pepper. Cook and stir for 1 minute more, stirring.

Transfer the Brussels sprouts to a bowl and sprinkle the reserved bacon over the top before serving it up.

CAST-IRON SKILLET CREAMED CORN

Serves 4–6

Prep time: 20 minutes
Cook time: 15 minutes

Canned creamed corn. Is. Not. Good. But for some reason, it's something people don't think to make at home. It's one of my favourite things that my mom makes and one of the most popular dishes we have at the restaurant. This side is traditionally hearty, usually calling for 240ml double cream. But here we lighten it up a bit by using 120ml double cream and 120ml chicken stock, keeping the smoky, sweet and creamy taste, but cutting out a few of the calories.

6 medium corn on the cob, husked

2 smoked streaky bacon rashers, sliced into 1cm pieces

1 shallot, very finely chopped

2 teaspoons chopped fresh thyme

sea salt and freshly ground black pepper

120ml double cream

120ml Homemade Chicken Stock (page 205)

15g butter

1 spring onion, thinly sliced

2 teaspoons sugar (optional)

Cut the kernels from the corn cobs and place in a medium bowl, making sure to use your knife to scrape off all the pulp and milk from the cobs into the bowl.

Cook the bacon in a cast-iron frying pan (skillet) set over a medium heat, stirring, for about 4 minutes until crisp. Transfer with a slotted spoon to a kitchen paper-lined plate and set aside.

Add the shallot to the same pan and sauté for about 2 minutes until softened. Stir in the corn with its pulp and the thyme and season with salt and pepper. Sauté for 2 minutes until the thyme is fragrant and the corn starts to turn lightly golden. Pour in the cream and stock and simmer for 5 minutes, or until the corn is just tender.

Transfer 240ml of the corn mixture to a food processor or blender and purée until it's smooth. Then place the puréed corn back into the pan and fold in the butter, reserved bacon and spring onion. Taste for seasoning, adding the sugar if your corn isn't sweet enough, and salt and pepper.

COOKING TIP

Puréeing some of the corn kernels adds a smooth texture to the creamed corn.

WILD RICE AND SWISS CHARD GRATIN

Serves 4–6

Prep time: 15 minutes (plus time to cook the rice)
Cook time: 50 minutes

What is a 'gratin'? It basically refers to any dish with a brown, crusty top that comes from baking or grilling cheese, butter or breadcrumbs. For many of us, that crusty bit is the most coveted part of the casserole. Like the edge of a brownie or the top of a muffin, it's where the goods are. I get tired of eating the same ol' rice, so here I give the starch staple a kick in the pants, transforming it from a low-brow side to a member of the 'upper crust' – a worthy accompaniment to Sunday's roast chicken.

180g long-grain and wild rice mix

450g Swiss chard, leaves removed from centre ribs and stems

55g butter, plus more for greasing

1 medium onion, finely chopped

sea salt and freshly ground black pepper

3 garlic cloves, finely chopped

2 teaspoons chopped fresh thyme

2 tablespoons plain flour

300ml full-fat milk

1 tablespoon dry sherry

dash of freshly grated nutmeg

45g panko breadcrumbs

25g Parmesan cheese, freshly grated

1 tablespoon olive oil

INGREDIENT NOTE

Swiss chard, a close relative of the beetroot, is available all year round and contains tons of nutrients. It's kind of bitter by itself, but when cooked into this dish, it adds another flavour dimension.

Preheat the oven to 180°C/gas mark 6. Grease a 2-litre baking dish with butter.

Cook the rice according to the packet instructions. Meanwhile, bring a large saucepan of salted water up to the boil. Trim off the tough bottoms of the Swiss chard stems. Slice the stems and ribs into 1cm pieces, add to the boiling water and cook for 2 minutes. Roughly chop the greens, then add them to the boiling water by handfuls and cook for a further 3 minutes until the stems and leaves are tender. Drain the greens in a colander and rinse with cold water to stop the cooking. Once cool, wrap the greens in a clean tea towel and gently squeeze out all the liquid. Unwrap and give the greens another chop.

Melt the butter in a large saucepan over a medium heat. Add the onion and sauté for about 5 minutes until softened. Season with salt and pepper, then stir in the garlic and thyme, cooking for about 1 minute, or until nice and fragrant. Sprinkle in the flour and cook, while stirring, for about 1 minute more. Pour in the milk, stirring constantly, and bring the mixture up to a simmer. Cook for 5 minutes, or until thick, then season with the sherry, nutmeg and another pinch of salt and pepper. Turn off the heat and fold in your cooked rice and Swiss chard.

Transfer the wild rice mixture to the prepared baking dish. Mix the breadcrumbs together with the Parmesan and oil in a small bowl. Evenly top the baking dish with the breadcrumb mixture. Bake for 25–30 minutes until bubbly and golden.

Normally, I'd rather eat more meatloaf and less potato. This dish is the one exception.

When I want to do a really special dinner for Brooke, I include this potato gratin, an easy-to-put-together side that tastes super-delicious. It's a once- or twice-a-year kind of dish because it's so heavy and rich. You can blame the cream and cheeses. Or you can thank the cream and cheeses. This goes great with roast beef fillet (page 91) or roast pork loin (page 80).

CREAMY POTATO GRATIN

Serves 4–6

Prep time: 10 minutes
Cook time: 1 hour 20 minutes

Preheat the oven to 180°C/gas mark 4. Grease a 2-litre baking dish with butter.

Add the cream, shallot, garlic, thyme and just a pinch of salt and pepper to a medium saucepan and bring to a simmer.

Add the potatoes to the pan, give them a stir and cook for 4 minutes, stirring on occasion, until you see the liquid thicken up. Remove and discard the thyme.

Pour half of the potato mixture into the prepared baking dish. Give the dish a shake to help the potato slices settle into an even layer. Sprinkle with salt and pepper and half of the Cheddar and Parmesan. Pour in the remaining potatoes and cream, then top with the rest of the Cheddar and Parmesan, along with one final seasoning of salt and pepper.

Cover tightly with foil, place on a baking tray and bake for 1 hour. Remove the foil and continue to bake for 10–15 minutes until golden and bubbly.

butter, for greasing

475ml double cream

1 shallot, very finely chopped

2 garlic cloves, very finely chopped

1 sprig of fresh thyme

sea salt and freshly ground black pepper

800g Yukon gold or Maris Piper potatoes, well scrubbed and cut crossways into 3mm-thick slices

115g mature Cheddar cheese, coarsely grated

25g Parmesan cheese, freshly grated

INGREDIENT NOTE

For a more grown-up flavour, substitute Gruyère for the Cheddar and add a dash of nutmeg.

COOKING TIP

Use a mandolin to create thin, even slices of potato. This dish can be made a day ahead and then reheated in a 180°C/gas mark 4 oven.

MOMMA'S ROASTED ACORN SQUASH WITH BROWN SUGAR

Serves 4

Prep time: 10 minutes
Cook time: 1 hour

Jack and I started a little garden together at the house and we were pretty certain we planted yellow squash. But instead, acorn squash miraculously appeared. Of course he expected me to do something really fabulous with his prize squash, but I didn't have a clue as to how to prepare it. Luckily Momma came to my rescue and showed me this simple recipe. This dish is both a little bit sweet and a little bit savoury; the fresh thyme kicks up the savoury element, balancing out the brown sugar and maple syrup. Jack ended up loving this recipe, but I can't help but think that pride for his home-grown squash had a little something to do with it.

2 medium acorn squash

70g butter, at room temperature

3 tablespoons soft light brown sugar

2 tablespoons real maple syrup

2 teaspoons chopped fresh thyme

sea salt and freshly ground black pepper

Preheat the oven to 200°C/gas mark 6. Line a baking tray with foil.

Slice each squash in half. Use a spoon to scoop out the seeds and discard. Arrange the squash, cut sides up, on the prepared baking tray.

Combine the butter, brown sugar, maple syrup, thyme and salt and pepper in a saucepan and bring to the boil. Remove from the heat and divide the melted butter mixture between the squash cavities, brushing some on the cut side of each squash. Bake for about 1 hour until the squash is tender when pierced with a fork.

ROASTED CAULIFLOWER WITH CRANBERRIES

Serves 4–6

Prep time: 15 minutes
Cook time: 20 minutes

If you've only had cauliflower steamed, there's a good chance you wouldn't go out of your way to make it at home. But there are a few simple steps that help maximise cauliflower's potential as a tasty side dish. Drizzling it with olive oil and roasting it in the oven draws out the flavour. Adding cranberries and almonds gives it sweetness, texture and colour. In the end it's really pretty, and more than that, it's delicious.

1 large head cauliflower (about 900g), cored and cut into florets

4 tablespoons olive oil

4 garlic cloves, roughly chopped

sea salt and freshly ground black pepper

60g dried cranberries

70g salted roasted almonds, chopped

2 tablespoons roughly chopped fresh parsley

1 tablespoon lemon juice

Preheat the oven to 230°C/gas mark 8.

Place the cauliflower on a baking tray and drizzle with the oil. Toss in the garlic and sprinkle with a big pinch of salt and pepper. Use your hands to mix it all together. Roast the cauliflower for about 20 minutes, flipping with a spatula halfway through cooking, until it's golden in spots and soft.

Transfer the cauliflower to a large serving bowl. While it's still hot, toss with the cranberries, almonds, parsley and lemon juice. Taste for seasoning, adding more salt and pepper if you think it needs it.

MOMMA'S MASHED SWEDE

Serves 6

Prep time: 10 minutes
Cook time: 50 minutes

It took me about 30 years to eat a rutabaga (swede) and I've been trying to catch up ever since. If you don't like 'em, you haven't had them done properly. My mom substituted them for mashed potatoes one night and I was surprised at their earthy-sweet flavour. They're creamy and delicious; underrated and underused. Farmers have been growing this veg – said to have evolved from a cabbage and a turnip – for more than 200 years in this country, but they're still a novelty at most American tables. Not mine.

3 medium (baseball-sized) swedes (about 675g), peeled and chopped

2 King Edward potatoes (about 675g), peeled and chopped

120ml full-fat milk

115g cream cheese, at room temperature, cut into chunks

55g butter, sliced into pats

sea salt and freshly ground black pepper

Add the swede to a large saucepan of cold salted water. Place over a medium-high heat and bring the water up to the boil. Reduce the heat to a simmer and cook for about 30 minutes. Add the potatoes to the pan and cook for a further 15–20 minutes until both the potatoes and swede are tender. Drain well. In the same pan over a medium heat, combine the milk, cream cheese and butter, stirring to melt, and seasoning with a big pinch of salt and pepper. Return the potatoes and swede to the pan and mash them up real well. Have a taste for seasoning and adjust as necessary.

GREEK SALAD COUSCOUS

Serves 6

Prep time: 15 minutes
Cook time: 5 minutes

There's a Greek restaurant we really like here in town and this recipe is like bringing those wonderful flavours home.

My brother started cooking with couscous a long time ago – way before it was ever trendy around here. And we'd make so much fun of him, mainly because we couldn't figure out what he was eating. A grain? Pasta? *Sand?* We weren't too far off. Couscous is actually a coarsely ground pasta made from wheat. And while colours and layers of flavour are important in most dishes, they're super-important in this one because, on its own, couscous doesn't taste like much. In this Greek-influenced dish, we're pulling out all the tricks by incorporating feta, fresh herbs, olives and cucumbers. The salad holds up really well as a second-day dish.

175g couscous

1 small shallot, finely chopped

1 cucumber, diced

190g baby plum tomatoes, sliced in half (a mix of red and yellow looks nice)

90g Kalamata olives, pitted and sliced in half

2 tablespoons chopped pepperoncini peppers (pickled mild green Italian chilli peppers)

75g feta cheese, crumbled

2 tablespoons chopped fresh parsley

2 tablespoons chopped fresh dill

3 tablespoons olive oil

2 tablespoons red wine vinegar

sea salt and freshly ground black pepper

Bring 475ml of lightly salted water to the boil. Stir in the couscous, cover with a lid and remove from the heat. Set a timer for 5 minutes. When the timer goes off, remove the lid, fluff the couscous up with a fork and transfer to a large mixing bowl. Leave the couscous to cool completely.

Once cool, add all the remaining ingredients and toss together really well. Taste for seasoning, adjusting with more salt and pepper, as necessary.

INGREDIENT NOTE

Pepperoncini are pickled peppers that pack a tangy bite. They add a little heat to this dish and some crunch.

CRUNCHY CURRIED RICE SALAD WITH APPLES AND SPRING ONIONS

Matthew is violently allergic to rice. His doctors say he may grow out of his allergy and I hope he does, because when it comes to food, that kid doesn't discriminate.

There are a million different ways to serve rice and one that I particularly like is rice salad. This is a flavourful side dish with a lot of texture and crunch. It holds well, so leftovers make the perfect next-day lunch; serve cold on a bed of rocket. The curry in this dish may be an acquired taste for some kids, but familiar ingredients such as raisins, apples and pistachios – some of Jack's favourite things – will encourage them to give this salad a try.

Heat the oil in a medium saucepan over a medium-high heat. Once it's hot, sprinkle the curry powder into the oil and cook, while stirring, for 30 seconds until fragrant. Stir in the rice and cook for 1 minute, then add the water and season with salt and pepper. Bring to the boil, reduce to a simmer, cover and cook for about 45 minutes until the rice is tender. Remove from the heat, sprinkle the raisins over the rice, cover and let the rice mixture steam for 15 minutes. Fluff up with a fork, then transfer to a large bowl to cool.

Add the celery, apple, spring onions and pistachio nuts to the cooled rice. Drizzle with the lime juice, season with salt and pepper and toss it all together.

INGREDIENT NOTE

Brown rice is a triple treat: it adds nice colour, a nutty flavour and it's more nutritious than white rice.

COOKING TIP

Toasting the curry powder brings out its pungent flavour. I like to use a mild curry powder to keep the heat in check.

Serves 6

Prep time: 15 minutes
Cook time: 1 hour

2 tablespoons olive oil

1 tablespoon curry powder

185g brown long-grain rice

475ml water

sea salt and freshly ground black pepper

80g raisins

1 celery stick, chopped

1 apple, cored and thinly sliced

4 spring onions, thinly sliced

40g roasted shelled pistachio nuts, chopped

juice of 1 lime

AUNT PEGGY'S CUCUMBER SALAD

Serves 6

Prep time: 15 minutes
Cook time: 20 minutes
(plus 20 minutes marinatin')

Aunt Peggy has served this fresh and tangy cold salad at every meal my whole life – every lunch, every dinner, every day. It's a classic recipe – not because my great aunt made it, but because *everybody's* great aunt made it. In my version, I cut down on the onion and added honey to sweeten up the dressing just a bit, making this salad more kid-friendly but every bit as memorable.

2 cucumbers (about 900g), peeled and thinly sliced

300g baby plum tomatoes, sliced in half

1/4 medium sweet onion, very thinly sliced

2 tablespoons chopped fresh parsley

sea salt and freshly ground black pepper

2 tablespoons cider vinegar

1 tablespoon olive oil

2 teaspoons honey

Toss together the cucumbers, tomatoes, onion and parsley in a large serving bowl. Sprinkle with a little salt and pepper.

Mix together the vinegar, oil, honey and salt and pepper in a small mixing bowl, whisking until the honey is dissolved. Pour the dressing over your salad and let it stand for about 20 minutes before serving to allow the flavours to develop.

BROCCOLI AND BACON TWICE-BAKED POTATOES

Serves 4

Prep time: 20 minutes
Cook time: 1 hour 30 minutes

Unless you just came out of the woods, one of these potatoes could easily be satisfying enough for your whole dinner.

I got my first hundred-dollar tip while working at a place called The Oyster Bar when I was in college. A guy and his two sons had just come out of the woods after hunting for three or four days and were starving. The owner of the place, Chuck, was really big on twice-baked potatoes, putting prawns or strips of sirloin steak and cheese in them rather than just on top. I discovered that extra step makes all the difference. I piled those potatoes on that man and his sons and they threw them down. That hundred dollars disappeared real fast, but the twice-baked-potato technique stuck. This is my version. Tips are always welcome.

4 large King Edward potatoes (350g each), well scrubbed and dried

1 head broccoli (280g), cut into florets

2 tablespoons olive oil

6 smoked streaky bacon rashers

3 spring onions, thinly sliced

115g mature Cheddar cheese, grated, plus more for serving

180ml sour cream

55g butter

sea salt and freshly ground black pepper

Preheat the oven to 220°C/gas mark 7.

Prick the potatoes with a fork. Place them on the top shelf of your oven and bake for 1 hour, or until tender. Meanwhile, place the broccoli on a baking tray, drizzle with the oil and roast for 18–20 minutes until tender-crisp. Lay the bacon on a foil-lined baking tray. Bake for 10–12 minutes, or until crisp. Transfer your bacon to a kitchen paper-lined plate to drain.

Turn your oven temperature down to 180°C/gas mark 4.

Once the bacon, broccoli and potatoes are cool to the touch, chop the bacon and broccoli and add to a mixing bowl. Slice off the top third of the potatoes and scrape any potato from the tops into the mixing bowl, discarding the skins. Using a spoon, scrape the flesh from the four potatoes into the mixing bowl (but keep the skins!). Add the spring onions, Cheddar, sour cream, butter and a big pinch of salt and pepper. Mash the potatoes, mixing everything together really well. Taste for seasoning, adding more salt and pepper if you need it. Put the potato mixture back into their skins. Place them on a baking tray and sprinkle each potato with a little more Cheddar. Bake for 20–25 minutes until the filling is hot and the cheese is melted.

BRAISED GREENS

Serves 6–8

Prep time: 20 minutes
Cook time: 30 minutes

We're getting back to the basics here. Old-fashioned Southern dishes are trending big time in fancy restaurants across the United States – even jumping the pond in some cases. But if y'all 'aren't from around here' and are unsure how to handle these massive, leafy greens, let me be your guide. Braising greens is a quick way to prepare this Southern staple, while still infusing them with the big smoky flavour they're known for.

450g kale

450g mustard greens

450g spring greens (substitute for Southern collard greens)

3 strips thick-sliced smoked streaky bacon, chopped

1 medium onion, chopped

3 garlic cloves, chopped

sea salt and freshly ground black pepper

475ml Homemade Chicken Stock (page 205)

1 tablespoon cider vinegar

1 tablespoon soft light brown sugar

1/8 teaspoon dried chilli flakes

Make sure your sink is nice and clean and then fill it with cold water. Strip the kale leaves from their stems, tear the leaves into pieces and toss the leaves into the water. Repeat with the mustard greens. To trim the spring greens, strip the leaves off the stems and add these to the sink as well. Agitate the water with your hands, making sure all the greens get cleaned. Remove the spring greens first; pile them up, roll into a cigar and slice into 1cm strips. Transfer all the greens to a large colander to drain.

Place the bacon in a large flameproof casserole dish and turn the heat to medium. Cook, stirring, for 5–6 minutes until the bacon is crisp and the fat is rendered. Transfer the bacon with a slotted spoon to a kitchen paper-lined plate and set aside.

Add the onion and garlic to the casserole dish and sauté for about 4 minutes until soft, seasoning really well with salt and pepper. Begin adding the greens in bunches, using tongs to toss them in the pan so that they wilt down a bit before adding another batch. Repeat until all the greens are in the pan. Season with another big pinch of salt and pepper, then pour in the stock, vinegar, sugar and chilli flakes. Bring the broth to the boil, then reduce the heat to medium, cover with a lid and braise for about 10 minutes. Remove the lid and cook for about 10 minutes more, tossing on occasion, until the greens are real nice and tender.

QUICK SAUTÉED MIXED VEGGIES AND HERBS

Serves 4

Prep time: 5 minutes
Cook time: 15 minutes

It's time to break out of the convenience-vegetable routine. When you need a quick and summery side dish, preparing this mix of fresh seasonal veg takes just a bit longer than it does to open a bag or turn a can opener, but it's so worth it. Luckily, both of our boys love vegetables, so Brooke and I make this recipe all the time. Like most gardens, ours gets overrun with courgettes and squash, which come in all at once. This is our favourite way to handle the harvest.

2 tablespoons olive oil

2 medium courgettes, chopped

1 medium yellow (summer) squash, chopped

sea salt and freshly ground black pepper

3 garlic cloves, roughly chopped

45g frozen peas, defrosted

2 tablespoons roughly chopped fresh basil

2 tablespoons roughly chopped fresh mint

Heat the oil in a large frying pan over a medium-high heat. Once it's hot, toss in the courgette and yellow squash and sauté for 8–10 minutes until the veggies are softened and lightly browned. Season the veggies with a good pinch of salt and pepper. Stir in the garlic and peas and cook for a further 2–3 minutes, or until the peas are heated through and the garlic is softened and fragrant. Toss in the herbs at the last minute and mix it up well.

COOKING TIP

Transform this into a main course by tossing in some cooked pasta at the last minute. I know you can't find *that* in a can.

The Payoff

Contrary to what some people may think, I didn't grow up finishing off dinner with a piece of Mom's Gooey Butter Cake every night, though that would've been pretty awesome. Dessert was actually something we reserved for special occasions, like birthdays or Christmas dinner. Our family saw sweets as a celebration food – something we really looked forward to and appreciated because it was a novelty at our table.

Because of this, I don't really have much of a sweet tooth, but I do like dessert when we're enjoying a meal with friends. By the end of the meal, everyone is relaxed, the conversation is easy and our bellies are full – but never too full for a taste of something sweet, like my brightly flavoured Best Lemon Tart (page 174) or the mouthwatering Peach and Blackberry Cobbler (page 177). Our kids like the idea of dessert, but rarely do they chow down. Instead, they excitedly enjoy a few bites and then go back to playing while the adults genuinely savour every bite.

While my boys love every dessert in this chapter, it was important to me to develop recipes sophisticated enough for a grown-up palate. Every dessert is baked, and almost all incorporate fruit in some form, a reflection of my personal bias. I prefer the flakiness of a baked dessert and the natural sweetness fresh fruit supplies. I don't gravitate towards overly gooey, greasy desserts, and we have so many wonderful peaches, lemons and strawberries around here – some grow in my backyard – it would be an oversight not to include them.

Note, when the need arises, I'm not above bribing my kids with dessert to get them to eat their dinner. A tempting sweet treat can serve as the proverbial carrot (cake) dangling on a stick, getting kids – or me – to do just about anything. But in my case, it's one hundred sit-ups.

BAKED APPLE TURNOVERS

Makes 8 pastries

Prep time: 10 minutes
Cook time: 30 minutes

I bet you wouldn't be shocked to know that my mom used to make deep-fried apple pies back when I was Jack's age. She would wrap apples and brown sugar in biscuit dough and drop it into a sizzling vat of oil. I loved those pies so much, but they didn't do much for my health. In our own house, Brooke and I have never deep-fried a thing. Not one time – and we've lived here for eight years. Instead, we do a lot of baking. By baking instead of frying, I can pass along this slightly revised family recipe, sharing the memories and flavours with the people I love but in a healthier way. I use fresh apples for the filling and just a little bit of brown sugar, then fold it up in ready-made puff pastry, which cooks up to be much lighter and flakier than a dense biscuit dough. Jack gets to enjoy the same dessert that I had when I was a fat little boy, except he's not a fat little boy.

30g butter

2 Gala apples, peeled, cored and chopped into 1cm cubes

2 Granny Smith apples, peeled, cored and chopped into 1cm cubes

160g soft light brown sugar

1 tablespoon plain flour, plus more for dusting

³/₄ teaspoon ground cinnamon

¹/₂ teaspoon ground ginger

¹/₈ teaspoon fine sea salt

1 medium egg

1 tablespoon water

500g ready-rolled puff pastry, defrosted if frozen

1 tablespoon granulated sugar for sprinkling

Melt the butter in a large sauté pan over a medium-high heat until it's foamy. Add the apples and cook, while stirring, for 3 minutes, or until they're slightly softened. Stir in the brown sugar, flour, cinnamon, ginger and salt, and continue cooking, stirring, for a further 3 minutes, or until the pan looks almost dry and the sugar is syrupy. Remove the apples to a bowl and leave to cool completely.

Preheat the oven to 200°C/gas mark 6 and adjust your oven shelves to the centre. Line two baking trays with baking parchment. Whisk together the egg and water in a small bowl and set it aside.

One at a time, very carefully unfold your sheets of puff pastry on a lightly floured work surface. Roll out each sheet to a 28cm square. Cut each sheet into four equal-sized squares and place them on the prepared baking trays. Brush the outside corners of each square with some egg wash and add one-eighth of the filling across the centre of each square, going from one corner to the other. Fold the top corner over the filling and press it to seal. Then fold the bottom corner over the last fold and press it to seal. (Two corners of the tart will remain open with the filling peeking out.) Repeat this step with the remaining squares of pastry. Brush the outside of each turnover with egg wash and sprinkle lightly with sugar. Bake for 20 minutes until puffy and golden. Allow the turnovers to cool a bit before serving.

COOKING TIPS

The filling can be made up to two days in advance – but I bet you won't be able to wait that long to use it.

Little cooks can help roll out the puff pastry, add the filling, brush with egg wash and sprinkle with sugar.

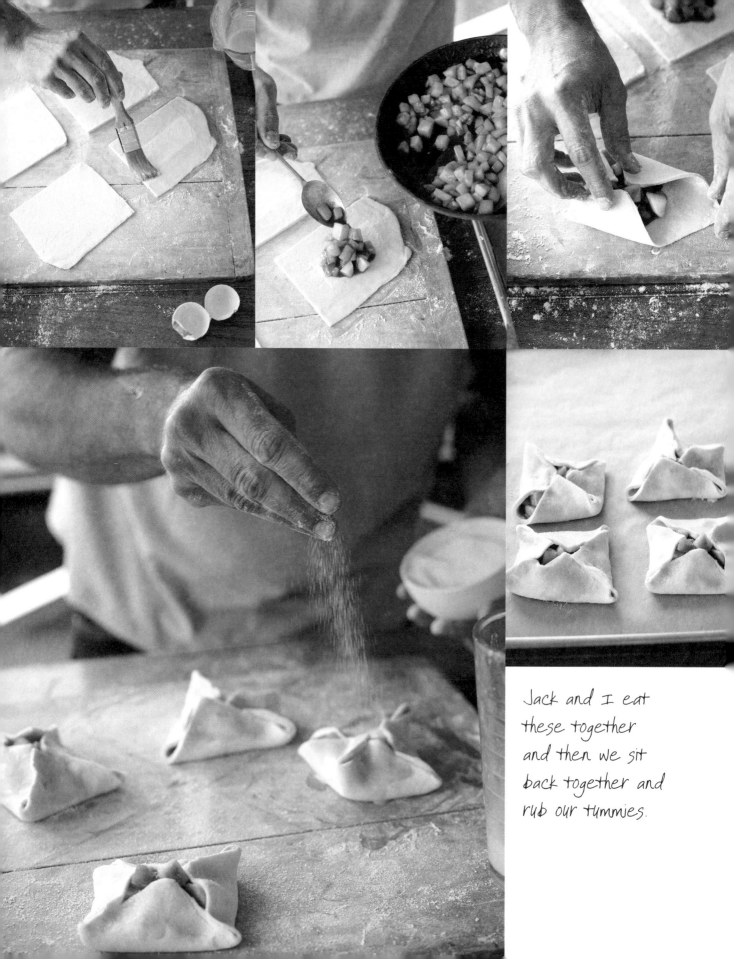

Jack and I eat
these together
and then we sit
back together and
rub our tummies.

To earn money to go to the Albany fair, Momma had Bobby and me sell pecans. She took us around the neighbourhood to all the pecan trees and we'd have to collect them into buckets. I always loved that fair, but hated pecans for a real long time. My relationship with pecans has since improved. We have four trees at our house, and when Jack was a bitty baby, I'd carry him around in my arms, pointing things out to him saying, 'This is grass. This is a tree. This is a pecan.' He got really excited about the pecans. It blew his mind that he could find food outside on the ground. Because pecans are such a big part of our lives, and Southern culture in general, I wanted to include a pecan pie recipe. This one riffs on tradition just a bit. A pretzel base and the palate-pleasing flavour of salted caramel are sure to land this divine dessert on your short list.

SALTED CARAMEL PECAN PIE WITH PRETZEL BASE

Serves 8

Prep time: 15 minutes
Cook time: 1 hour 5 minutes

Preheat the oven to 180°C/gas mark 4.

Add the pretzel crumbs, flour, sugar and melted butter to a medium bowl and stir until combined. Dump the crumb mixture into a 23cm deep-dish pie plate and press it evenly around the base and sides of the pan. Place the pie plate on a baking tray to catch drips and bake for 10 minutes until firm.

Combine the brown sugar, golden syrup, butter pieces and sea salt in a medium saucepan over a medium heat and bring it up to the boil while stirring. Remove from the heat and cool. Whisk in the eggs, then switch to a wooden spoon to stir in your pecans. Pour the mixture into the pretzel base and bake for 50 minutes. Cool the pie completely before serving.

140g pretzels, whizzed in a food processor or crushed with a rolling pin to crumbs

2 tablespoons plain flour

3 tablespoons granulated sugar

100g unsalted butter, melted, plus 85g cut into pieces

230g soft dark brown sugar

330g golden syrup

1 tablespoon flaky sea salt (preferably Maldon)

3 medium eggs, lightly beaten

230g pecan nuts, chopped

INGREDIENT NOTE

I like to use a flaky sea salt like Maldon, which has a more intense flavour than if you use a table salt. You'll taste the difference.

 ## COOKING TIP

This pie can be made a day ahead. In fact, you want to prepare the pie with enough time for it to cool and set up. If not completely cool, pecan pies can be runny.

JACK'S FAVOURITE BLONDIES

Makes two dozen 5cm blondies

Prep time: 10 minutes
Cook time: 40 minutes

When I was growing up, my Great Aunt Glyniss made blondies every year at Thanksgiving. They've been everybody's favourite in this family at some point or another, and right now they're Jack's. See, he doesn't like chocolate, which kind of limits the number of baked goodies we can treat him to. But Great Aunt Glyniss's recipe seems to do the trick. It's not too sweet, but the toffee combined with the toasted pecans offers a buttery and nutty flavour that my son really enjoys.

170g unsalted butter
480g soft light brown sugar
250g plain flour
2 teaspoons baking powder
³/₄ teaspoon fine sea salt
2 medium eggs
2 teaspoons pure vanilla extract
150g toffees, broken into pieces
85g toasted pecan nuts, chopped

Preheat the oven to 180°C/gas mark 4. Adjust the shelves to the centre of the oven.

Line a 23cm x 33cm baking tin with foil, leaving a 5cm overhang for easy removal after baking. Spray the foil lining with non-stick baking spray.

Melt the butter in a large saucepan over a medium-high heat. Once it's melted, stir in the brown sugar and cook, stirring, until it's all combined. Remove the mixture from the heat and leave it to cool for 5 minutes. Meanwhile, whisk together the flour, baking powder and salt in a medium bowl.

Stir the eggs into the cooled sugar and butter mixture one at a time until they're well incorporated. Stir in the vanilla and then add the flour mixture to the saucepan, mixing to combine. With a rubber spatula, fold in the toffee and chopped pecans.

Spread the batter in the prepared tin. Bake for 35–40 minutes until golden brown and a cocktail stick inserted into the centre comes out clean. Leave to cool for 30 minutes. Using the overhanging foil, remove the blondies from the tin and slice them into 24 squares.

SUMMER STRAWBERRY OAT CRISP

Serves 6

Prep time: 15 minutes
Cook time: 30 minutes

When strawberry season arrives in the South, I pack up the family and drive to this beautiful place called Ottawa Farms, just a short drive outside of Savannah. The 700-acre farm has been around since 1878 and hosts an annual Strawberry Festival complete with music, pig races, a corn maze, cow train rides and an alligator show – I'm telling you, this is real country fun. We never miss the festival – or its trademark strawberry ice cream – but we also visit the farm all through the spring to pick berries. When we have more strawberries than we can use, we freeze them so we can warm up to this sweet and crunchy summery dessert in the autumn and winter months.

900g strawberries, hulled and halved (quartered if very large)

100g granulated sugar

3 tablespoons plain flour

1 tablespoon lemon juice

1/8 teaspoon sea salt

OAT TOPPING

95g old-fashioned porridge oats

35g plain flour

105g soft light brown sugar

85g unsalted butter, at room temperature

70g salted roasted pistachio nuts, chopped

good vanilla ice cream or Homemade Whipped Cream (page 209)

Preheat your oven to 180°C/gas mark 4. Spray a 1.5-litre square baking dish with some non-stick baking spray.

Toss together the strawberries, sugar, flour, lemon juice and salt in a large bowl, then spread the mixture in the prepared baking dish.

Combine the oats, flour, brown sugar, butter and pistachios in a medium bowl, crumbling it all together with your hands. Evenly sprinkle the oat topping over the berries, then pop the baking dish in the oven and bake for 30 minutes until the strawberries are soft, the filling is bubbling and the topping is lightly golden.

Let the crisp cool for 30 minutes to allow the filling to thicken up. Serve it with a big ol' scoop of vanilla ice cream or whipped cream on top.

CRACKLY OATMEAL COOKIES

Makes 4 dozen cookies

Prep time: 10 minutes
Cook time: 15 minutes

The world is divided into two kinds of people – those who like their cookies chewy and those who like them crisp. I definitely fall into the former category. This cookie puffs up during baking and then falls as it cools, giving the tops a nice crackled appearance, while staying perfectly gooey on the inside.

115g unsalted butter, at room temperature

115g white vegetable fat

320g soft light brown sugar

100g granulated sugar

2 medium eggs

2 teaspoons pure vanilla extract

250g plain flour

1 teaspoon bicarbonate of soda

1 teaspoon ground cinnamon

3/4 teaspoon fine sea salt

225g quick-cooking oats

80g raisins

SUGAR AND CINNAMON TOPPING

100g granulated sugar

1 teaspoon ground cinnamon

Preheat the oven to 180°C/gas mark 4 with the shelves in the centre.

Combine the butter, vegetable fat and both sugars in the bowl of a freestanding mixer fitted with a paddle attachment. Beat on a medium-high speed for about 5 minutes until fluffy. Add the eggs, one at a time, beating well after each, then beat in the vanilla.

Combine the flour, bicarbonate of soda, cinnamon and salt in a medium bowl. Gradually add the dry ingredients to the wet ones, beating until combined. Using a rubber spatula, fold in the oats and raisins.

To make the topping, combine the sugar and cinnamon in a medium bowl. Roll the dough into golf ball-sized balls. Gently roll the balls through the sugar and cinnamon mixture. Place the cookies on a baking tray, leaving 5cm of space between each ball of dough. Bake the cookies for 12–14 minutes until they're lightly golden.

Leave the cookies to cool on the tray for 2 minutes, then remove from the tray and cool completely on wire racks.

LEMON SHORTBREAD COOKIES

Makes 4 dozen cookies

Prep time: 10 minutes (plus 1 hour's chilling time)
Cook time: 20 minutes

Shortbread is one of those rare things that both kids and adults love. There aren't a lot of bells and whistles to this crumbly cookie – it's just a straight-up buttery biscuit that melts in your mouth. The addition of the lemon and the sanding sugar gives it something special without tampering with its timeless goodness.

225g unsalted butter, at room temperature

120g icing sugar

250g plain flour

$^3/_4$ teaspoon fine sea salt

1 tablespoon finely grated lemon zest (from 1 large lemon)

1 tablespoon lemon juice

pale yellow sanding sugar (optional)

Put the butter and icing sugar in the bowl of a freestanding mixer fitted with a paddle attachment. Beat for about 5 minutes until light and fluffy, scraping down the sides of the bowl with a rubber spatula once or twice.

Whisk together the flour, salt and lemon zest in a medium bowl. While the mixer is running, add half of the flour mixture to the creamed butter by large scoopfuls. Once the flour is incorporated, squeeze in the lemon juice, then add the remaining half of the flour mixture. The dough should stick together when pinched.

Set a large piece of greaseproof paper in front of you. Place the dough on the centre of the paper and form it into a log about 30cm long. Roll the dough up in the paper, making a square log shape, and twist the ends of the paper to secure. Chill in the refrigerator for 1 hour.

Preheat the oven to 180°C/gas mark 4. Then line a baking tray with baking parchment.

Cut the chilled dough into 5mm-thick slices and place them on the prepared baking tray about 2.5cm apart. Sprinkle the cookies with sanding sugar, if you like. Bake for 18–20 minutes until the cookies are light golden brown around the edges. Cool them for 5 minutes on the baking tray, then remove to a wire rack to cool completely.

FRESH FRUIT AMBROSIA WITH SHREDDED COCONUT

Serves 6

Prep time: 15 minutes
Cook time: 10 minutes

Momma had a plastic storage container that magically appeared at Christmas when she made her ambrosia salad. It should've held enough salad to feed 20 people, but it only fed the four of us because we loved it so much. A lot of folks add whipped topping, mayonnaise or marshmallows to their salad, but I like how Mom always kept it clean and simple: nothing but heaped spoonfuls of fruit and coconut.

45g sweetened shredded coconut (look for Baker's Angel Flake online, or use desiccated coconut sweetened with a little icing sugar)

60g pecan nuts, roughly chopped

3 navel oranges, peeled and segmented

2 medium blood oranges, peeled and segmented

1 medium ruby red grapefruit, peeled and segmented

$^{1}/_{2}$ medium ripe pineapple, peeled, cored and diced

75g jarred maraschino cherries, drained and sliced in half

1 medium banana, peeled and sliced

Preheat the oven to 180°C/gas mark 4.

Spread the coconut and pecans out on a baking tray and toast them in the oven for about 7 minutes until the coconut is golden brown. Transfer to a plate to cool.

Toss the navel and blood oranges, grapefruit, pineapple, cherries and banana together in a large bowl. Scoop up any juice that you may have lost on your work surface from segmenting the citrus and add it to the bowl as well. Sprinkle in the coconut and pecans and toss it all together.

 ## COOKING TIPS

You can make this up to a day ahead of time. Just leave out the banana until just before you serve, otherwise it will turn brown and soften. Then sprinkle with toasted coconut – you don't want to lose that crunch. Feel free to thinly slice the citrus into rounds instead of segmenting.

YES, A JELLY SALAD

Serves 6–8

Prep time: 10 minutes
Cook time: 10 minutes (plus
4 hours' chilling time)

A cookbook coming out of the South without a jelly salad would be like Saturday morning without cartoons. Total blasphemy. The only thing worse would be if you've never actually had a jelly salad.

Calling this dish a 'salad' is a bit of a misnomer. It's really an amped-up strawberry cheesecake, but I can't ever wait until after the meal to enjoy it, so I insist on making it something we serve alongside the main course. Brooke makes jelly salad every year at Christmastime and brings it to Mom's house. As a testament to how good it is, I always cut back on my mom's dishes because I'm saving room for that salad. (But you didn't hear that from me.)

BASE

225g salted pretzels

140g unsalted butter, melted

50g sugar

225g cream cheese, at room temperature

150g sugar

225ml whipping cream, whipped until stiff

675g fresh strawberries, hulled and sliced

175g powdered strawberry jelly, from a sachet

475ml boiling water

475ml cold water

Preheat the oven to 180°C/gas mark 4. Spray a 23cm x 33cm baking dish with non-stick baking spray.

Put the pretzels in the bowl of a food processor and whizz them until you're left with chunky crumbs.

In a medium bowl, mix together the pretzels, melted butter and sugar. Firmly press the pretzel mixture into the base of the prepared dish and bake for 10 minutes. Leave to cool completely – about 30 minutes.

Add the cream cheese to a freestanding mixer fitted with a whisk attachment and beat until nice and smooth. Sprinkle in the sugar and beat again for about 3 minutes until light and fluffy. With a rubber spatula, fold in the whipped topping and spread it over the cooled pretzel base, making sure to seal all the edges. Layer the sliced strawberries on top and place in the refrigerator to chill for 1 hour.

Place the jelly in a medium bowl and pour the boiling water over it, stirring to dissolve. Stir in the cold water. Gently pour the gelatine over the chilled salad. Refrigerate for about 4 hours until the salad is completely set and chilled.

APPLE CINNAMON STREUSEL CAKE

Serves 8

Prep time: 15 minutes
Cook time: 50 minutes

I'm not a real big dessert guy, but the ones that I lean towards always involve some kind of baked fruit. This soft, moist apple cake has a sweet and crunchy topping that reminds me of cinnamon toast, only better – like 85g of butter better. I use American Honeycrisp apples, but any sweet, crisp apple will do.

Preheat the oven to 180°C/gas mark 4. Spray a 20cm square baking dish with non-stick baking spray.

First make the streusel. Combine the brown sugar, flour, cinnamon and salt in a medium bowl, whisking together until well blended. Use a fork to cut in the butter, then switch to your fingers to really crumble the streusel all together. Once it's all combined, stir in the walnuts. Pinch together some of the topping to create some large crumbles for varying texture. Set aside the topping while you make the cake.

In a separate medium bowl, whisk together the flour, baking powder, cinnamon, allspice and salt.

Add the butter and sugar to the bowl of a freestanding mixer fitted with a whisk attachment and beat for about 5 minutes until the mixture is light and fluffy. Scrape down to the bottom of the bowl with a rubber spatula halfway through beating to ensure it's all coming together. Beat in the eggs, one at a time, making sure the first is well blended before adding the second, then beat in the sour cream and vanilla. Add the flour mixture by scoopfuls and mix until well incorporated. Turn the mixer off and stir in the diced apples. Your batter should be thick.

Pour the batter into the prepared dish, smooth the top and sprinkle with the streusel. Bake for 50–55 minutes until a skewer inserted into the centre comes out clean. Leave to cool for about 30 minutes before serving.

STREUSEL

70g soft light brown sugar

45g plain flour

1 teaspoon ground cinnamon

$1/4$ teaspoon fine sea salt

85g unsalted butter, chilled and cut into small cubes

65g chopped walnuts

190g plain flour

1 teaspoon baking powder

1 teaspoon ground cinnamon

$1/2$ teaspoon allspice

$1/2$ teaspoon fine sea salt

115g unsalted butter, at room temperature

150g sugar

2 medium eggs, at room temperature

180ml sour cream

1 teaspoon pure vanilla extract

$1^1/2$ medium Gala or other sweet, crisp apples, cored, peeled and diced

THE BEST LEMON TART

Serves 8

Prep time: 20 minutes
Cook time: 50 minutes

There may be lots of different tarts in the world, but to me there's just a lemon tart. That's why it's the best.

This sweet and citrusy dessert is perfect when you want a lot of bang for your buck. The freshly squeezed lemon juice paired with a nutty almond pastry case packs flavour into every bite. You won't need a big slice to get the full effect, but you will ask for another just because it's that good.

PASTRY

30g flaked almonds

160g plain flour, plus more for dusting

60g icing sugar

1/4 teaspoon fine sea salt

140g unsalted butter, chilled and sliced

1 medium egg, lightly beaten

LEMON CURD

250g granulated sugar

180ml freshly squeezed lemon juice (from 4–5 lemons)

1/4 teaspoon fine sea salt

4 medium eggs plus 1 large yolk

85g unsalted butter, chilled and sliced

icing sugar for serving (optional)

To make the pastry, toast the almonds in a small dry frying pan over a medium heat, stirring, for about 3 minutes until just slightly blond. Transfer to a plate to cool completely.

Add the flour, icing sugar and salt to a food processor and pulse a few times to mix and break up any lumps in the sugar. Add the cooled almonds and pulse again for 30 seconds until they are broken up. Add the butter and pulse until the dough forms small clumps. Add the beaten egg and pulse in long increments until the dough comes together, bunched up into a few balls.

Lightly dust your work surface with flour. Use non-stick baking spray to prepare a 23cm tart tin with a removable base. Transfer the dough to the work surface. Lightly knead it a few times to incorporate all the dry ingredients, and then form it into a flat disc. Press the dough into the base of the prepared tart tin and up the sides. Chill for 30 minutes in the freezer. Preheat the oven to 180°C/gas mark 4.

Once chilled, remove the tart from the freezer and place it on a baking tray. With a fork, prick the base of the tart all over to prevent the dough from puffing up while it bakes. Line the tart with baking parchment and place baking beans on top (dried beans will work at a pinch). Bake for 25 minutes. Remove the tart from the oven, remove the paper and baking beans and bake the pastry case for a further 2 minutes until lightly golden. (If the pastry has puffed up during baking, press it back down with the back of a spoon.)

Meanwhile, make the lemon curd. Whisk together the granulated sugar, lemon juice, salt and eggs in a medium, heavy-based saucepan. Turn the heat to medium and cook, while stirring, for about 8 minutes until the curd is thick. (If you're worried about how to tell whether the curd is fully cooked, it's done when it reaches 77°C.) Whisk in the butter, piece by piece; the curd will loosen up slightly. Pour the mixture into a large measuring jug.

Carefully pour the lemon curd into the pastry case. (Do not overfill.) Bake the tart for about 10 minutes until the custard is set. Remove the tart from the oven and leave it to cool completely in the tin. Remove the sides from the tart tin and slice the tart. Sprinkle with icing sugar to serve.

Any recipe where ice cream functions as a garnish has got to be good.

Peach cobbler has been a staple at our restaurant for more than 25 years. One day, I decided to shake things up by throwing in some fresh blackberries and it turned out that we all really liked those two flavours together. And now this is my family's go-to cobbler.

PEACH AND BLACKBERRY COBBLER

Serves 6–8

Prep time: 15 minutes
Cook time: 55 minutes

Preheat the oven to 180°C/gas mark 4. Adjust the shelf to the centre of your oven.

Add the butter to a 3-litre baking dish and place it in the oven just until the butter melts. Then quickly remove from the oven and set aside.

Combine the peaches, blackberries, 200g of the sugar and the water in a medium saucepan and mix well. Bring the mixture to the boil, reduce the heat to a simmer and cook for 10 minutes until the peaches and berries are soft and the liquid is syrupy.

Whisk together the flour, baking powder, salt and remaining 200g sugar in a medium bowl. Slowly whisk in the milk and cinnamon, if using, mixing until smooth. Pour the batter over the butter in the baking dish, and then spoon the fruit and syrup on top. Bake for 45 minutes. Serve warm with a big scoop of vanilla ice cream.

INGREDIENT NOTE

I recommend fresh, but you can also use frozen fruit as well. I like baking with yellow peaches because they are slightly less sweet than white peaches and have a more intense flavour.

115g unsalted butter, melted

4 peaches, peeled, stoned and sliced (about 675g)

175g fresh blackberries

400g sugar

120ml water

190g plain flour

$2^{1}/_{4}$ teaspoons baking powder

$^{1}/_{2}$ teaspoon fine sea salt

300ml full-fat milk

$^{1}/_{2}$ teaspoon ground cinnamon (optional)

'ARE YOU THIRSTY? WANT A SNACK?'

'Are you thirsty? want a snack?'

When I became a parent, there was so much that I wasn't prepared for – things that only experience can teach you, like the incredible lengths you'll be willing to go to to get your child to sleep. I wore a path around the house, circling it with a baby in my arms, singing the only verse to 'Hush, Little Baby' that I knew, over and over and over again.

It's this relentless repetition that surprised me the most.

As Jack has got older, I've stopped walking in circles and, to Brooke's relief, learned to offer more than just the 'mockingbird', but I still repeat myself on a daily – no, hourly – basis. 'Do you need to use the bathroom?' 'Please don't run with scissors.' 'Please don't paint _____.' (Insert 'the sofa', 'the dog' or 'your brother'.) And, my personal favourite, 'Are you thirsty? Do you want a snack?'

I've discovered that kids don't announce that they're hungry or thirsty until they're borderline starving or dehydrated, at which point they lose the ability to use their words and instead resort to undesirable, non-verbal cues such as crying or fainting. To avoid this scenario, I find myself repeatedly offering my boys satisfying snacks and drinks like the homemade Cheesy Cheddar Puffs (page 194) and fresh-squeezed Savannah Minted Lemonade (page 182) included in this chapter.

I'd like to think I'm able to separate my roles as parent and host, but the truth is, there's some overlap. I've never had a guest in my home ask for something to eat or drink: I don't give them the chance. As soon as you cross our threshold, you're going to be bombarded with offers of food and drink until you finally accept. Southerners are just as relentless as they are hospitable, y'all.

Sweet tea and candied pecans are certainly tradition around here, but I also like to offer guests something outside the Southern sphere, so to speak. My recipes for candied orange peel, American biscuits and even collard green wontons are easy to do and leave a big impression. Many of the drinks in this chapter incorporate fresh fruits and herbs, and all of the adult drinks that include alcohol can be modified for children who want to feel grown up. Likewise, the kid-friendly drinks can be easily dressed up with a jigger of this or that. In the end, nobody goes hungry or thirsty on my watch.

I just can't promise that the dog won't get painted.

SAVANNAH MINTED LEMONADE

Serves 12

Prep time: 10 minutes
Cook time: 5 minutes

There's no better way to quench your thirst in the summer than a tall glass of freshly squeezed lemonade packed with ice. I've got a Meyer lemon tree in the garden with these big, beautiful lemons that come in all at once, so I make a point of squeezing pitchers full of them when that happens. The cool hint of mint makes this lemonade even more refreshing – and it adds some nice colour. It's the perfect porch drink.

1.9 litres cold water

400g sugar

45g loosely packed fresh mint leaves, plus more for garnish

475ml freshly squeezed lemon juice (from 9–10 lemons), plus additional lemon slices for serving (optional)

In a medium saucepan, combine 475ml of the water, the sugar and mint, gently twisting the leaves to release the essential oils. Turn the heat to medium-high and bring to the boil, stirring until the sugar dissolves. Reduce the heat and simmer for 2 minutes, then remove from the heat and cool completely, letting the mint steep in the hot syrup.

Strain the sugar syrup into a pitcher, discarding your mint leaves. Stir in the lemon juice and remaining cold water. Tear up a few fresh mint leaves and add them to the pitcher. Refrigerate until chilled. Serve your lemonade in tall, ice-filled glasses garnished with mint leaves, and lemon slices if you like.

COOKING TIP

Before squeezing the lemons, give 'em a roll on the kitchen work surface to help release the juice.

STRAWBERRY SIPPER

Serves 5

Prep time: 15 minutes (plus 1 hour marinatin')
Cook time: zero

Whenever Jack sees adults drinking colourful cocktails with paper umbrellas and fruit garnish, he thinks he's missing out. So, at restaurants we sometimes order him a classic Shirley Temple – soda water and cherry juice with a maraschino cherry floating on top. It's good, but it doesn't hold a candle to this combination of strawberries, limes and mint. Because the garnish is really what makes a drink seem adult to Jack, this Strawberry Sipper is a win-win for both of us: he gets to enjoy a fresh fruit 'mocktail', and I can enjoy a grown-up version by adding some tequila.

2.7kg fresh strawberries, hulled and quartered

juice of 3 limes (about 6 tablespoons)

20 fresh mint leaves, plus additional sprigs for serving

65g caster sugar

240ml tequila (optional)

soda water

Combine the strawberries, lime juice, mint and sugar in a blender and pulse to create a chunky purée. Transfer to a small glass jug and stir in the tequila, if using. Place in the refrigerator for 1 hour until well chilled and the flavours have had a chance to marry together (if time allows; sometimes we can't wait!).

Pour about 120ml of the strawberry mixture over each ice-filled rocks glass, top with soda water and give a little stir. Garnish each drink with a mint sprig.

INGREDIENT NOTE

For an interesting variation on this sipper, use basil in place of the mint and vodka in place of the tequila.

What makes this a 'Savannah' lemonade? The 400g of sugar. If you ever have our sweet tea, you'll understand.

When you have friends coming over, this is a great make-ahead drink recipe because you don't have to muddle the drinks one by one.

FROZEN GEORGIA PEACH MARGARITA

Makes 6 drinks

Prep time: 5 minutes
Cook time: zero

Texans know a thing or two about cattle ranching and drilling for oil, but they also have a long and loving relationship with beer. So, I guess it shouldn't have surprised me when a friend of mine from there made me a 'Texas Margarita' with, you guessed it, beer. It adds another layer of flavour that partners well with the bite of the limeade and tequila. I'm willing to give credit where it's due, but as soon as I added peaches, this margarita crossed into Georgia territory.

240ml tequila

175ml limeade concentrate, defrosted but still chilled

240ml beer

450g peeled, stoned and frozen peaches

240g ice cubes

coarse salt (optional)

Combine all of the ingredients in a blender (except the salt, of course) and blend until smooth. Serve your margaritas in salt-rimmed glasses, if desired.

INGREDIENT NOTE

You can go ahead and use the whole can of limeade if you prefer your margaritas sweeter.

PARTY PUNCH

Serves 15

Prep time: 5 minutes (plus freezing time)
Cook time: zero

Punch is an easy and cost-effective alternative to made-to-order cocktails when you have a festive gathering. The fresh fruit ice ring adds an element of fun to the punch that's both pretty and functional – it keeps your drink cold without watering it down.

2 limes, sliced

500g fresh raspberries

1 litre pomegranate juice

2 litres ginger ale, chilled

1.8 litres limeade, chilled

2–3 bottles prosecco (optional)

First make your ice ring. Place the sliced limes and raspberries on the bottom of a ring cake tin. Cover the fruit with cold water by 10cm. Freeze overnight until the ice forms a solid ring.

When you're ready to serve, combine the pomegranate juice, ginger ale and limeade in a 7.5-litre punch bowl. To unmould the ice ring, run the bottom side of the cake tin under warm water to loosen it. Carefully place the ice ring in the punch bowl, fruit side up.

Offer the bottles of chilled prosecco next to the punch, if the adults want to top off their drinks.

PEPPERMINT HOT COCOA

Serves 4

Prep time: 10 minutes
Cook time: 10 minutes

Hot cocoa is such a satisfying drink, but part of what makes it so magical is the fact that we don't have it every day. It's a treat we get to enjoy on a cold winter's afternoon when nothing else will warm us, or our spirits. The peppermint gives my recipe a little something extra – a festive twist on tradition – and a generous heap of homemade whipped cream beats chewy marshmallows every time.

700ml full-fat milk

250ml double cream

225g good-quality milk chocolate chips

85g round hard peppermint sweets, crushed, plus 4 more crushed sweets for serving

Homemade Whipped Cream for serving (page 209)

Heat the milk and cream in a large saucepan over a medium heat. Once it's warm, add the chocolate and crushed peppermints and whisk for about 5 minutes until the chocolate is melted and the peppermint is dissolved. Serve the cocoa in mugs and top each with a big dollop of whipped cream and a sprinkle of the extra crushed peppermint sweets.

MULLED CIDER

Serves 4

Prep time: 5 minutes
Cook time: 25 minutes

If the temperature drops to a frigid 10°C, adults should feel free to add a shot of bourbon.

The South can get really cold in the winter – like 10 degrees C. And while that might sound like a beach day to those living further north, you've got to understand that more than two decades of sunshine can change a man. To warm up, Brooke and I make a batch of this spicy and fragrant mulled cider that the boys also can enjoy when they need to defrost.

1.2 litres apple cider

2 cinnamon sticks

5cm piece fresh ginger, sliced into rounds

1 star anise

3 x 5cm strips lemon peel

$1/8$ teaspoon ground cloves

Combine all of your ingredients in a large saucepan over a medium-high heat. Bring up to the boil, then reduce the heat to a low simmer and gently simmer for 20 minutes. Remove from the heat and leave to steep for 5 minutes. Serve the cider in mugs and get cosy.

THE DEEN FAMILY EGGNOG

Serves 15

Prep time: 25 minutes (plus chilling time)
Cook time: zero

My grandmother Hiers made eggnog every year at Christmas – a family tradition my mom kept up with. We kids were so fascinated by it because it looked so delicious – all thick and creamy, like what I imagined a sweet-cream-butter milkshake would look like. But we could never drink any 'cause, just like my grandmother, Momma put bourbon in it. It's not an everyday drink; it's not even an every-so-often drink. But in my family, it's the holiday drink of choice.

6 medium eggs, separated

150g sugar

950ml full-fat milk

240ml bourbon (optional)

475ml double cream

1 tablespoon pure vanilla extract

freshly grated nutmeg for serving

Put the egg yolks in the bowl of a freestanding mixer fitted with the whisk attachment and beat until combined. While beating, slowly add 100g of the sugar to the egg yolks and continue beating for about 4 minutes until the mixture is thick and light yellow in colour. Whisk in the milk and, if using, the bourbon.

In a second bowl, beat the egg whites until they're frothy, then slowly add the remaining 50g sugar, beating until stiff peaks appear.

In a third bowl, beat the cream and vanilla together until stiff peaks appear, then gently fold into the eggnog. Chill in the refrigerator for 2–4 hours before serving with freshly grated nutmeg, to taste.

INGREDIENT NOTE

If you like the flavour of bourbon but not the fuzzy head that comes with it, you can exchange it for a tablespoon of rum extract.

At one of our favourite bakeries here in town, Back in the Day Bakery, owners Cheryl and Griff Day make these incredible American biscuits with bacon cooked into them, except they call them 'biscones'. For somebody like me from South Georgia, anything that looks like a biscuit and tastes like a biscuit is a *biscuit*. The end. This recipe is inspired by Back in the Day's.

BACON CHEDDAR 'BISCUITS'

Makes 12 biscuits

Prep time: 20 minutes
Cook time: 15 minutes

Preheat the oven to 200°C/gas mark 6 and then line a baking tray with baking parchment.

Cook your bacon over a medium-high heat in a large frying pan until crisp. Remove it with a slotted spoon to a kitchen paper-lined plate to cool. Set aside 1 tablespoon of the bacon dripping in a small bowl.

Whisk together the flour, baking powder, sugar, salt, bicarbonate of soda, spring onion and cooled bacon in a large bowl. Using a fork, cut the butter into the dry ingredients until the mixture looks like coarse crumbs, then stir in the cheese.

Dig a well in the centre of your flour and slowly stir in the buttermilk and reserved bacon dripping, just until the dough is sticky but still a bit crumbly on the bottom of your bowl. Dust your work surface with some flour, dump the dough onto your surface and knead three or four times until all the loose crumbs come together. Pat into a rough round shape with your hands and press the dough to a 2cm thickness. With a 5.5cm round biscuit cutter, cut out 12 biscuits, making sure you do not twist.

Place the biscuits on the prepared baking tray, allowing 5cm of space between each one. Brush the tops with some buttermilk. Bake the biscuits for 15 minutes until the tops are lightly golden, rotating the pan halfway through baking.

225g smoked streaky bacon, chopped

225g plain flour, plus more for dusting

1 1/2 teaspoons baking powder

1 teaspoon sugar

1/2 teaspoon fine sea salt

1/2 teaspoon bicarbonate of soda

1 spring onion, thinly sliced

55g unsalted butter, chilled and cut into cubes

85g Cheddar cheese, grated

180ml buttermilk, plus more for brushing

CORNY CORNBREAD

Serves 6–8

Prep time: 15 minutes
Cook time: 25 minutes

Cornbread without kernels of corn is like an apple pie without the apples – I just don't get it. But it's amazing to me how often cornmeal passes for corn in many cornbread recipes. Not this one. I'm husking corn from the cob to give this recipe some authenticity. The result is a dense, moist cornbread that's the perfect pairing for Chilli (page 42), Black-eyed Peas (page 199) or any other savoury Southern dish.

85g butter

1 corn on the cob, husked and kernels removed from the cob

3 spring onions, sliced

sea salt and freshly ground black pepper

150g yellow cornmeal

125g plain flour

2 tablespoons sugar

1½ teaspoons baking powder

½ teaspoon bicarbonate of soda

115g Cheddar cheese, grated

350ml buttermilk

2 medium eggs, lightly beaten

Preheat your oven to 220°C/gas mark 7 and adjust the shelf to the centre of the oven. Spray a 20cm baking dish with non-stick baking spray.

Heat the butter in a large frying pan until melted and foamy. Add the corn kernels and spring onions and sauté over a medium-high heat for about 2 minutes until the corn is soft. Season with a nice hit of salt and pepper, then remove from the heat and set aside.

Whisk together the cornmeal, flour, sugar, baking powder, bicarbonate of soda and ½ teaspoon salt in a large bowl. Add the cheese and toss to combine with your hands. Transfer the sautéed corn mixture to a separate large bowl, using a rubber spatula to scrape all the butter and bits into the bowl. Add the buttermilk and eggs and stir to combine.

Make a well in the centre of the dry ingredients, pour the buttermilk-corn mixture into the well and then stir until only just combined.

Pour the batter into your prepared baking dish and bake for 30–35 minutes, or until a skewer inserted in the centre of the bread comes out clean. Leave the cornbread to cool before serving it up.

COLLARD GREEN WONTONS

Serves 8–10

Prep time: 25 minutes
Cook time: 35 minutes (plus frying time)

We developed this recipe at the restaurant and loved it so much we served these wontons at Mom's wedding reception. Besides being really pretty, they bring together two otherwise distinct cultures – the Far East and Down South – in an interesting and tasty way, marrying a flaky shell with creamy bacon-infused greens on the inside. It's a proven winner at the restaurant and a recipe you can easily bring to your next party.

225g spring greens (substitute for Southern collard greens)

1 dried chilli

4 smoked streaky bacon rashers, chopped

1/2 medium sweet onion, finely chopped

sea salt and freshly ground black pepper

115g goat's cheese, softened

475g wonton wrappers

groundnut oil for frying

To prepare the greens, strip the green leaves off the stems and toss them into a clean sink filled with cold water. Agitate the water with your hands to make sure the greens get clean. Pile the leaves up, roll them into a cigar and slice into 1cm-thick strips.

Bring a large flameproof casserole dish of salted water plus the chilli to the boil. Add the greens and simmer for 20–25 minutes until tender. Remove your greens with a slotted spoon to a bowl to cool. Discard the chilli. Once cool, gently squeeze all the excess liquid from the greens.

Cook the bacon in a large frying pan for 12 minutes until it's rendered enough fat to cook the onion. Add the onion and sauté for 4–5 minutes until tender and soft and the bacon is crisp. Season with a pinch of salt and lots of black pepper. Transfer the bacon and onion to the bowl with the greens to cool.

To make the filling, put the goat's cheese and greens mixture in a food processor and blend until well combined.

To assemble the wontons, add 1 heaped teaspoon of the filling to the centre of a wonton wrapper. Wet the edges of the wrapper with your finger, then fold the wrapper over and press to seal the edges, making sure to press out any air. Repeat with the remaining filling and wontons; you should have about 40 wontons total.

To cook the wontons, heat 5cm of oil in a high-sided frying pan until it reaches 190°C on a deep-frying thermometer. Fry the wontons in batches for about 2 minutes until they're golden brown and crisp. Drain on a kitchen paper-lined baking tray. The filling will be piping hot, so let the wontons cool for a few minutes before serving.

INGREDIENT NOTE

Fresh out of wonton wrappers? You can also serve the filling with crackers as an unexpected greens dip.

CHEESY CHEDDAR PUFFS

Makes 26–30

Prep time: 5 minutes
Cook time: 35 minutes

These are best served warm and with drinks. Carton juice or bottled beer; it's your call.

Cheese straws are really big around here – they're the Southern equivalent of beer nuts. For this recipe, I've reinvented them as 'puffs' so they look super kid-friendly (especially in a lunch box) but have a grown-up bite to 'em. That's cayenne pepper, but you can back off on that if your kids are, well, babies.

240ml full-fat milk

115g butter, chilled and cut into chunks

2 teaspoons fine sea salt

$^1/_2$ teaspoon freshly ground black pepper

125g plain flour

pinch of cayenne pepper

4 medium eggs, at room temperature

145g mature Cheddar cheese, grated

Preheat the oven to 190°C/gas mark 5. Line two baking trays with baking parchment or silicone baking mats and lightly coat with non-stick baking spray.

Combine the milk, butter, salt and pepper in a large saucepan over a medium heat, stirring, until the butter is melted. Sprinkle in the flour and cayenne, and stir vigorously with a wooden spoon for about 2 minutes until the dough comes together in the base of the pan, moves away from the sides of the pan and looks shiny and smooth. Transfer the dough to the bowl of a freestanding mixer fitted with the whisk attachment and leave to cool for 1 minute.

Beat in the eggs, one at a time, then add 115g of the cheese and beat until a smooth dough forms.

Drop the dough by tablespoons onto the prepared baking tray, leaving about 5cm of space between each ball. Sprinkle with the remaining 30g cheese.

Bake for 30 minutes, rotating the trays halfway through, until puffed and golden brown. Serve 'em up warm.

COOKING TIPS

In order to work quickly, it's best to prepare and measure all of your ingredients before starting this recipe. Jack loves to help me make these puffs because, like cookies, it's a drop-dough recipe.

CANDIED ORANGE PEEL

Makes about 80g

Prep time: 10 minutes
Cook time: 55 minutes

Everyone loves candy, as in sweets, but many people are turned off by the idea of fussing around with thermometers, moulds and scorching-hot syrups that rival molten lava. But this is not that kind of candy. It's a really easy recipe that I picked up when I was a kid and have made a million times since.

COOKING TIP

Around Christmastime, I like to put this candied peel out in little dishes, but it also makes for a nice decoration on just about any dessert – after all, even the most decadent chocolate torte can handle a little dressing up.

2 navel oranges
200g sugar
180ml water

Line a baking tray with baking parchment. Use a vegetable peeler to remove the peel from the oranges. Try to remove just the peel and not too much of the bitter white pith. Slice the peel into 5mm-thick strips and toss them in a saucepan of cold water. Bring up to the boil, then reduce the heat to a simmer and cook for 10 minutes. Drain the peel and leave it to cool.

Add 150g of the sugar and the water to the same saucepan and bring to the boil, all the while stirring to dissolve the sugar. Turn the heat to low, add the orange peel and simmer gently for 45 minutes, stirring occasionally, until the mixture is very syrupy.

With tongs, transfer the peel to the prepared baking tray, using the tongs to separate the pieces if they've stuck together. (Don't use your hands – the zest will be real hot.) Leave the candied peel to cool for 5 minutes. Sprinkle the remaining 50g sugar over the tops to coat. Leave the peel to dry for 30 minutes and then store in an airtight container for up to 2 weeks.

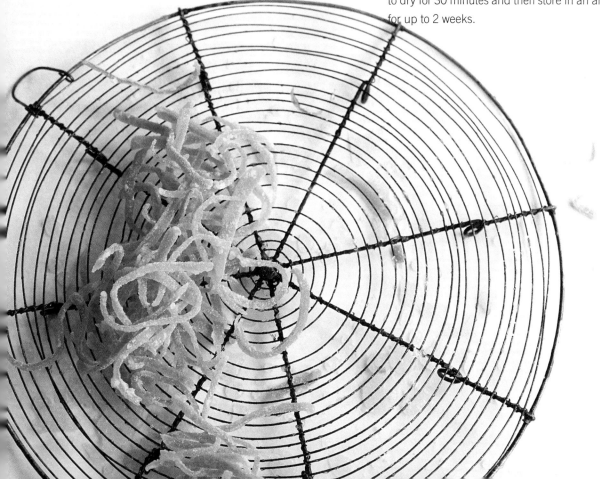

Date Night With Old Sparky

Just to clarify, 'Old Sparky' isn't Brooke's nickname for me – yet. It's what Southerners call the electric chair. See, we have this habit of making things sound better than they actually are. 'Chitlins' for example, sound like cute, baby 'chits', but they're actually fried pig intestines.

So, when I got to thinking about my favourite meal of all time, I asked myself the age-old question: if I was facing certain death, what would I want my last meal to be?

For some, this question is a bit like being asked to pick your favourite child. I enjoy so many different kinds of foods. If I didn't, I certainly wouldn't be where I am today, writing this book for y'all. Instead, I would've followed my dreams of becoming a writer of a different sort, and I'd probably be living on Mom's couch right now.

So how can I choose just one meal?

As it turns out, the answer, for me, is quite simple. And I don't even have to wait to be sentenced to death to enjoy it, because it's the same meal Momma makes every New Year's Day: fried pork chops, collard greens with corn dumplings, black-eyed peas, lacy hoecakes and cane syrup and butter on white bread – it's the stuff Southern boys are made of.

A favourite meal transports us back in time. For some, it may be the dish they associate with a special moment, like an engagement or milestone birthday. For others, it's an incredible restaurant meal they enjoyed while holidaying in someplace memorable and magical, like New York City or Paris. For me, it's the traditional meal by which I greet each New Year and all of the possibilities it holds.

But because this is my last meal, I would make one revision: I would eat three times the amount I do every January 1st. Besides, I'll be gone long before heartburn sets in.

COLLARD GREENS WITH CORNMEAL DUMPLINGS

Serves 4–6

Prep time: 20 minutes
Cook time: 1 hour 45 minutes

It's a myth that greens have to be bathed in butter to taste good. In this recipe, they absorb their full flavour from the chicken wings (we use smoked turkey wings). Plus, because they're rich in vitamins C and K, and soluble fibre, they're really nutritious. The cornmeal dumplings are just a bonus – golden nuggets nestled on a bed of greens.

2.4 litres water

350g roast barbecue chicken wings

1 tablespoon hot sauce

1 teaspoon sea salt

30g butter

450g spring greens (substitute for Southern collard greens)

CORNMEAL DUMPLINGS

150g yellow cornmeal

125g plain flour

1 tablespoon sugar

1 teaspoon sea salt

30g butter, melted

1 medium egg, lightly beaten

2 tablespoons finely chopped sweet onion

1 tablespoon finely chopped fresh parsley

Combine the water, chicken wings, hot sauce, salt and butter in a large flameproof casserole dish over a medium-high heat. Bring to the boil, then reduce to a simmer and cook for 1 hour.

Strip the leaves off the greens and toss them into a clean sink filled with cold water. Agitate the water with your hands to make sure the greens get clean. Pile the leaves up, roll into a cigar and slice into 1cm-thick strips. Add the greens to the pot with the wings and simmer for 20 minutes, stirring occasionally, until tender. Reserve 240ml of the cooking liquid in a small bowl for your dumplings. Using tongs, remove the greens to a serving bowl and cover to keep warm. Discard the wings; set the broth aside.

To make the dumplings, whisk together the cornmeal, flour, sugar and salt in a medium bowl. Stir in the reserved cooking liquid, butter, egg, onion and parsley.

Bring the reserved greens broth back up to a low simmer and carefully drop the dumpling batter into it, 1 tablespoon at a time. Gently shake the pot instead of stirring with a spoon so that the dumplings won't fall apart. Simmer the dumplings lightly for 20–25 minutes until cooked through. Serve the greens and dumplings with some of the broth ladled over the top.

BLACK-EYED PEAS WITH HAM HOCKS

Serves 6

Prep time: 20 minutes
Cook time: 2 hours 25 minutes (plus overnight soaking and chilling)

Ever heard of osso buco? That's the fancy name Italians use for ham hock, when really they should just call it 'black-eyed-peas seasoning'.

I'm always shocked when I have customers who come into the restaurant and say they've never tasted black-eyed peas (beans). Once they try them, they're always surprised by how incredible they can taste. The secret ingredient here is the ham hock – it goes into all of our Southern-prepared vegetables, from collard greens to runner beans. It's where the flavour comes from. I don't care where you grew up, once you've enjoyed this traditional dish you won't wait until you're south of the Mason-Dixon line to make it for yourself.

450g dried black-eyed beans (peas)

1 large ham hock (450g)

2 tablespoons olive oil

1 medium onion, chopped

sea salt and freshly ground black pepper

3 garlic cloves, chopped

2 sprigs of fresh thyme

1 bay leaf

1 small dried chilli

1 glug hot sauce, to taste

Pick through the beans to remove and toss out any small stones or shrivelled-up ones. Place the beans that passed inspection in a colander, rinse them well under cold water, then add them to a big bowl and cover with cold water. Cover the bowl with clingfilm and then leave them to soak overnight.

Carefully cut the ham hock into three separate pieces, working around the bone. Put them in a large flameproof casserole dish and add enough cold water to cover plus 2.5cm. Bring to the boil, then reduce to a moderate simmer and cook, uncovered, for $1\frac{1}{2}$ hours, or until the ham hock is tender. Leave to cool to room temperature, then store the ham stock with the ham hock in the fridge overnight.

The next day, heat a large saucepan over a medium-high heat. Add the oil, and once hot, stir in the onion and sauté for about 5 minutes until softened. Season with salt and pepper, then stir in the garlic and sauté for about 1 minute until fragrant. Drain the beans and add them to the pan, along with the reserved ham hock and ham stock. Toss in the thyme, bay leaf and chilli. Bring the mixture to the boil, then reduce to a low simmer and cook for 45 minutes, stirring on occasion. Transfer the ham hock to a chopping board to cool slightly. Once it's cool enough to handle, give the meat a rough chop and stir it back into the pan, discarding any bones. Taste for seasoning and adjust as necessary with salt, pepper and a glug of hot sauce.

COOKING TIP

These might seem a bit of work: both the beans and the ham stock should be prepared the day before to allow for overnight soaking. But these wouldn't be real Southern black-eyed peas without ham hocks. Believe me, it's worth the effort!

MOMMA'S FRIED PORK CHOPS

Serves 4

Prep time: 5 minutes
Cook time: 10 minutes

This is a loosen-my-belt meal. I don't have it often, but when I do, I do it right.

Momma's fried pork chops are my favourite. The end.

475ml rapeseed oil

4 x 5cm-thick bone-in pork chops, 225–280g each

sea salt and freshly ground black pepper

125g plain flour

Line a baking tray with kitchen paper. Pour the oil into a large, high-sided frying pan; you want the oil to be about 1cm deep. Heat the oil to 180°C over a medium-high heat.

Season the pork chops on both sides with salt and pepper. Put the flour in a baking dish and season with salt and pepper, whisking until combined. Dredge the pork chops in the flour on both sides and shake off any excess. Carefully add the pork chops to the hot oil and cook for 5 minutes on each side until they're golden brown and cooked through. Once they come out of the pan, drain them on the prepared baking tray and season again with a little pinch of salt.

LACY HOECAKES

Serves 6

Prep time: 5 minutes
Cook time: 40 minutes

You wouldn't eat mashed potatoes without gravy; the same goes for hoecakes and cane syrup.

Hoecake, a Southern term for what other regions may call johnnycake or cornbread, got its name from the way it was sometimes prepared by field hands. They placed the batter on a hoe and held it over an open flame to cook. Today we use a skillet (frying pan) or griddle, but I wouldn't be above using a shovel at a pinch – that's how much I love it. Cornbread is such a big part of Southern cuisine that we've got about 15 different ways to make it. I like this version because the cakes are so thin and delicate, they look like lace.

225g cornmeal

1 teaspoon sea salt

540ml water

groundnut oil for frying

golden syrup for serving (substitute for Southern cane syrup)

Whisk together the cornmeal and salt in a medium bowl. Pour in the water and whisk vigorously for about 3 minutes until the batter is really smooth and very loose.

Heat 1½ tablespoons oil in a large, well-seasoned cast-iron frying pan over a medium-low heat. Pour about 80ml of the batter into the hot oil and quickly and gently press the centre of the cake out about 13cm across. Cook for 5 minutes until the edges are browned and lacy, then use a thin spatula to flip it, being very gentle with the edges. Cook the other side for 5 minutes until lightly golden brown with lacy edges, then transfer to the prepared baking tray to drain. Whisk the batter again before making the next hoecake, and add another 1½ tablespoons of oil to the pan.

Repeat until you have finished cooking all of the batter, and serve immediately with a drizzle of syrup on top.

INGREDIENT NOTE

A traditional Southern sweetener, cane syrup is very sweet, thick and syrupy, of course

COOKING TIPS

The batter should look more like that of a crêpe than a pancake batter – the thinner, the better. A non-stick frying pan will do here instead of a cast-iron one.

ODE TO DAD'S DESSERT

Serves 4

Prep time: 5 minutes
Cook time: zero

I saw my daddy eat this every night for 20 years. He would cut cold butter into cane syrup and spread it on white bread. It was the best thing in the world to him and that's reason enough for me to love it, but the truth is, it actually tastes incredible, too.

55g cold butter
80g golden syrup
4 slices white bread

Place the butter in a small bowl and drizzle it with the syrup. Cut the butter into the syrup and then spread it evenly on the bread.

Bits and Pieces

I have a lot of friends who are artists, and I'm so blown away by their incredible ability to dream up something in their heads and then transfer that idea onto paper. But talking to them, I've realised that drawing is a lot like cooking. To be an artist, you first have to master the basics, gaining an understanding of colour, shape and line. From there, you can move into more non-representational forms. The point is that there is a foundation on which artists build their craft, before they can ever create something beautiful and unique. In the immortal words of Bob Ross, there are such things as 'happy accidents', but those are few and far between.

Cooking is a similar art form. Learn the most basic techniques and made-from-scratch sauces and marinades and it will open the door to hundreds of different dishes. The possibilities are endless, but you still have to put one foot before the other in order to pass through that door.

This chapter provides a starting point for home cooks looking to move beyond the jar. Most of the recipes are guidelines for creating your basic sauces and dressings. Others are building blocks for more specific items, like homemade baby food (page 212), apple sauce (page 211) and steel-cut oatmeal (page 204). And then there are the compound butters. How do you improve on something like butter? The secret is on page 209 – and you'll be surprised by just how easy it is.

This chapter could just as well be the opening for this book – these foundation recipes are so essential. But instead, they're tucked away in the back, like a wonderful secret waiting to be discovered.

NIGHT BEFORE STEEL-CUT OATMEAL

Serves 8

Prep time: 5 minutes
Cook time: 10 minutes (plus standing overnight)

If I can prepare breakfast on Sunday night for Thursday morning and get my kids out the door with most of their clothes on, I consider myself Parent of the year.

If you have kids, oatmeal is probably something you've become reacquainted with – that, and craft paste. These two things, however, should never be confused. That's why I like steel-cut oats. They're better for you, really stand up to cooking and don't double as a binding agent. But the best part about this recipe is that you can make it ahead of time, keeping it in your fridge throughout the week. To bring it back to life, just reheat it, cutting it with a little cream. We like to set out a buffet of oatmeal 'fixin's' alongside so that Jack can add brown sugar plus his choice of nuts and berries.

15g butter

320g pinhead (steel-cut) oatmeal

1.6 litres water

$^1/_2$ teaspoon sea salt

240ml full-fat milk

optional toppings: berries, nuts, brown sugar, maple syrup, mashed bananas, peanut butter

Melt the butter in a medium saucepan over a medium heat. Stir in the oats and toast them, while stirring, for about 3 minutes until they smell nice and nutty. Stir in 1.4 litres of the water and your salt and bring the oats to the boil. Once they've reached the boil, turn off the heat, give a final stir, cover with a lid and call it a night.

The next morning at breakfast time, remove the lid and stir in the milk and remaining water, and slowly bring the oats back up to a simmer, stirring well. Serve the oatmeal hot with whatever toppings you like. Cool down and then wrap up any remaining oats in a covered container and place in your refrigerator. Reheat the oats in a saucepan or microwave for breakfast throughout the week.

HOMEMADE CHICKEN STOCK

Makes about 1 litre

Prep time: 5 minutes
Cook time: 2 hours

It would be a waste to throw out the leftovers from a roast chicken dinner because I know I can turn that skin and bones into an entire litre of chicken stock to use for weeks to come – and even longer if I freeze it. This flavourful recipe is just another example of how a little homemade touch can make a big difference in your dishes.

1 leftover roast chicken carcass

1 large onion, peeled and cut into chunks

1 carrot, scrubbed and cut into chunks

1 celery stick, cut into chunks

3 sprigs of fresh parsley

1 bay leaf

1 teaspoon black peppercorns

2.8 litres cold water

Use kitchen scissors to cut the chicken carcass into four pieces. Place the chicken in a large saucepan with the onion, carrot, celery, parsley, bay leaf and peppercorns. Cover with the water and bring it up to a simmer, then reduce the heat to low. Cook for 2 hours, skimming the top to remove fat and foam on occasion. (You don't want to boil your stock; instead, just let it bubble gently.)

Leave the stock to cool, then strain and discard the solids. The stock will keep for 1 week in a covered container in your fridge, or up to 6 months in your freezer.

COOKING TIP

Alternatively, you can add all the ingredients to a slow cooker, top with the lid and cook on low overnight.

WINTER GREEN PESTO

Makes about 375g

Prep time: 15 minutes
Cook time: 5 minutes

Everyone is familiar with basil pesto (see page 104), but in the winter months when the price for fresh basil is at a premium, I opt for a seasonal substitution. Kale makes a beautiful, bright pesto that I use in a bunch of different ways. I'll mix it in with some pasta for dinner, spoon it on a baked sweet potato for lunch, spread it on my sandwiches or swirl it into some sautéed vegetables for a quick side dish. We use pistachios, Jack's favourite, but you can use walnuts, boosting the health factor. Yep, it's a power pesto.

225g kale, stems removed, leaves torn

2 garlic cloves, peeled

70g salted roasted pistachio nuts

50g Parmesan cheese, finely grated

120ml extra-virgin olive oil

freshly ground black pepper

Bring a large saucepan of salted water to the boil. Add the kale by handfuls and boil for about 3 minutes until soft. With a slotted spoon, transfer to a colander, rinse with cold water and drain well. Leave to cool. Reserve 60ml of the cooking water.

Once the kale is cool enough to handle, squeeze out all the excess water with a clean tea towel. Add the kale to the bowl of a food processor along with the garlic, pistachios, Parmesan, oil and a big pinch of pepper. Pulse until smooth, then add the reserved water to thin out the pesto.

COOKING TIP

If serving your pesto with pasta, save yourself some time by reusing the blanching water to cook the pasta.

BASIC TOMATO SAUCE

Makes about 1.5kg

Prep time: 10 minutes
Cook time: 25 minutes

Make a large pot of this sauce at the start of the week, and all you have to come up with each night is a protein and a pasta to create a wide variety of hearty meals, from primavera, prawn pasta and aubergine parmigiana, to beefy 'mac' or spaghetti and meatballs. Let this fresh and easy sauce be your platform for a headfirst dive into Italian cooking.

4 x 400g cans whole peeled tomatoes with their juices

3 tablespoons olive oil

1 medium onion, finely chopped

sea salt and freshly ground black pepper

3 garlic cloves, very finely chopped

$1/8$ teaspoon dried chilli flakes

20g fresh basil leaves, roughly chopped

Add the tomatoes to a blender and purée until smooth.

Heat the olive oil in a large saucepan over a medium-high heat. Add the onion and sauté for about 5 minutes until it's softened and just beginning to turn lightly golden brown. Season the onion with salt and pepper. Stir in the garlic and chilli flakes and continue to cook, while stirring, for 1 minute. Pour in the tomatoes, bring 'em to a simmer and cook on a medium heat, stirring on occasion, for 20 minutes. Turn off the heat, season your sauce with salt and pepper and stir in the basil.

Refrigerate leftovers in an airtight container for up to 1 week, or freeze for up to 3 months.

EASY WHITE SAUCE

Makes about 700g

Prep time: 5 minutes
Cook time: 15 minutes

From this basic starting point, you can go in a lot of different directions with this sauce. For example, mix in 115g grated Cheddar cheese and you have a creamy cheese sauce that you can use to top steamed veggies and satisfy picky eaters, or add lots of freshly ground black pepper and turn this sauce into a perfect pepper gravy to smother on American-style biscuits (page 189).

60g butter

30g all-purpose flour

600ml full-fat milk, warmed

sea salt and freshly ground black pepper

$1/8$ teaspoon cayenne pepper

Melt the butter in a medium saucepan over a medium heat. Once the butter is melted, sprinkle in the flour and then stir for about 3 minutes until the flour is toasted and pasty blond in colour. Slowly whisk in the milk, season with salt and pepper and bring the sauce up to the boil. Reduce the heat to a simmer, and cook, stirring on occasion, for 10–15 minutes until thickened and the sauce coats the back of a spoon. Add the cayenne, and adjust any additional salt and pepper to taste.

PIMENTO CHEESE

Makes about 500g

Prep time: 5 minutes
Cook time: zero

Most family secrets are best kept under wraps, but not this one. In the name of improving pimento sandwiches around the world, I'm willing to let you in on our secret ingredient: cream cheese. This is one recipe where I encourage you to 'double dip': In addition to being one of the most popular sandwiches The Bag Lady ever sold, this spread doubles as a creamy dip.

115g cream cheese, at room temperature

115g mayonnaise

sea salt and freshly ground black pepper

230g mature Cheddar cheese, grated

45g drained and chopped jarred Spanish piquillo peppers or roasted red peppers

celery sticks or crackers for serving

Combine the cream cheese and mayonnaise in a large bowl, then season with salt and pepper. Beat with a hand mixer until the dip is completely smooth and light. Add the Cheddar and pimentos and beat again until the mixture is well combined.

Serve with celery or crackers, or transfer to an airtight container and refrigerate for up to 1 week. If you're making this dip ahead of time, remove it from the refrigerator about half an hour before serving so that it can soften up.

INGREDIENT NOTE

For bigger flavour, add 1 tablespoon grated onion and $1/2$ teaspoon garlic powder. If you like a little heat, add a few dashes of hot sauce.

SIMPLE JAM-JAR VINAIGRETTE

Makes 240ml

Prep time: 5 minutes
Cook time: zero

This basic vinaigrette packs a big flavour punch and isn't weighed down with too much oil or sugar. I like to sprinkle it over fresh leafy greens or sauté vegetables in it. It's also the perfect, light marinade for chicken or white fish.

1 garlic clove, smashed

1 tablespoon Dijon mustard

60ml red wine vinegar (or your choice of vinegar)

180ml olive oil

pinch of sugar

sea salt and freshly ground black pepper

Add all of the ingredients to a jam jar and shake it up. Taste for seasoning and adjust as necessary with salt and pepper. Store in an airtight container in the fridge for up to 1 week.

INGREDIENT NOTE

Unleash your inner chemist, playing with different vinegars and seasonings to change up the flavour:

Add 2 teaspoons of chopped herbs for a fresh flavour.
Add 1 tablespoon of mayonnaise for a creamier dressing.
Use lemon juice instead of vinegar.
Add 1 small very finely chopped shallot for extra zing.

HOMEMADE BUTTERMILK RANCH DRESSING

Makes about 180ml

Prep time: 5 minutes (plus optional chilling)
Cook time: zero

President Jimmy Carter told me that his favourite dessert has always been cornbread dipped in buttermilk. I'm a fan of President Carter, but I just can't say the same for buttermilk, y'all. Cornbread is, however, delicious with ranch dressing.

Whenever there was just a bit of mayonnaise left, my mom would make ranch dressing, shaking it up in that very same jar. Now, anytime I'm scraping out the last of the mayonnaise, I think about her, and more times than not, I'll get inspired to throw together this creamy ranch dressing.

120ml buttermilk

55g mayonnaise

1 tablespoon white wine vinegar

1 garlic clove, finely chopped

2 tablespoons thinly sliced chives

1/2 teaspoon onion powder

1 teaspoon hot sauce

sea salt and freshly ground black pepper

Add all of the ingredients to a jar and shake it up. If time permits, cover the dressing and refrigerate for 1 hour to allow the flavours to develop. Store in an airtight container in the fridge for up to 1 week.

HOMEMADE ZESTY FRENCH DRESSING

Makes 240ml

Prep time: 5 minutes (plus optional chilling)
Cook time: zero

My parents always kept a ton of blue cheese dressing at the house, but it wasn't exactly a kid magnet. French dressing, on the other hand, is pretty much universally loved by the three-foot-and-under crowd. Some adults may think this tangy, bright-orange dressing isn't as 'fancy' as a balsamic something-or-other, but I bet they've got a bottle stashed away at home. Everyone does. Like my ranch dressing, this recipe is simple to make and holds up really well. You'll also find that it tastes better than the bottled stuff because it's made with ingredients you can pronounce, with one exception: 'Worcestershire'.

4 tablespoons rapeseed oil

4 tablespoons tomato ketchup

3 tablespoons sugar

3 tablespoons white wine vinegar

1 tablespoon mayonnaise

1 tablespoon water

1 teaspoon paprika

1 teaspoon Worcestershire sauce

1 teaspoon Dijon mustard

sea salt and freshly ground black pepper

Combine all of the ingredients in a jam jar, seal the top and shake it up. Store in an airtight container in the fridge for up to 1 week.

COOKING TIP

Assemble this dressing an hour before you serve so that the flavours have time to come into their own.

HOMEMADE WHIPPED CREAM

Makes about 270g

Prep time: 5 minutes
Cook time: zero

I always thought whipped cream should be a dish of its own rather than a topping. It's fluffy, flavourful and completely addictive. But I suppose because it's so rich, a little bit goes a long way. In fact, it goes so far as to fool your guests – pile a dollop onto a shop-bought fruit pie and it'll then taste like a homemade dessert. Or try spooning it over the top of my Peach and Blackberry Cobbler (page 177), Summer Strawberry Oat Crisp (page 167) or Peppermint Hot Cocoa (page 186).

240ml double cream

3 tablespoons icing sugar

1 teaspoon vanilla extract

Pour the cream into the bowl of a freestanding mixer fitted with the whisk attachment, turn the speed to medium and whip. Once the cream starts to thicken up, add the sugar and vanilla and beat until medium-firm peaks form.

COOKING TIP

Whip the cream in a bowl that you've chilled in the freezer. I've always used a metal bowl, but you could do it in a glass bowl as long as it's well chilled beforehand. When your whipped cream starts to form peaks, stop. If you whip it too long, you'll have something else altogether: butter. As much as I like butter, I don't want to top my pie with it.

COMPOUND BUTTERS

Making a compound butter is a fancy move that's really simple – a 'trick your friends and impress your neighbours' sort of thing. You can really incorporate any flavour into the butter that you want, but I've come up with some foolproof recipes that pair real well with chicken, fish and steak, especially when they're simply prepared. As soon as the butter melts, it infuses its flavours into the dish, giving it a leg up.

BLACKBERRY COMPOUND BUTTER

Serves 8

Prep time: 5 minutes (plus freezing time)
Cook time: zero

Bobby and I discovered this recipe when we were on the road about ten years ago and we were surprised by how much we liked the berry flavour. It seems like it would be best spread on a muffin or Danish, but it actually pairs really well with a savoury steak.

115g unsalted butter, at room temperature

2 heaped tablespoons blackberries

1 teaspoon finely chopped fresh thyme

sea salt and freshly ground black pepper

Add the softened butter and berries to a medium bowl and mix vigorously, crushing the berries with the back of a rubber spatula. Add the thyme, season with salt and pepper and mix again to combine. Place tablespoons of the butter down the centre of a square piece of baking parchment and roll it up into a log, twisting the ends to secure. Place the butter in the freezer for 30 minutes to firm it up. To use, slice the butter into rounds to top steak, chicken or fish.

HERB COMPOUND BUTTER

Serves 8

Prep time: 5 minutes (plus freezing time)
Cook time: zero

You can use any herbs you like, but this is my favourite combination to serve on barbecued or grilled chicken.

115g unsalted butter, at room temperature

1 tablespoon each finely chopped fresh parsley, chives and tarragon

1 garlic clove, very finely chopped

sea salt and freshly ground black pepper

Place the softened butter in a medium bowl and mix in the parsley, chives, tarragon and garlic. Season the butter with salt and pepper and mix again to combine. Arrange tablespoons of the butter down the centre of a square piece of baking parchment and roll it up into a log, twisting the ends to secure. Place the butter in the freezer for 30 minutes to firm it up. To use, slice the butter into rounds to top steak, chicken or fish.

LEMON COMPOUND BUTTER

Serves 8

Prep time: 5 minutes (plus freezing time)
Cook time: zero

You're going to put lemon and butter on your fish anyway, so you might as well give this tasty trick a try.

115g unsalted butter, at room temperature

finely grated zest of 1 lemon

1 garlic clove, very finely chopped

sea salt and freshly ground black pepper

Place the softened butter in a medium bowl and mix in the lemon zest and garlic. Season with salt and pepper and mix again to combine. Arrange tablespoons of the butter down the centre of a square piece of baking parchment and roll it up into a log, twisting the ends to secure. Place the butter in the freezer for 30 minutes to firm it up.

 COOKING TIP

Sometimes I like to roast a fillet of fish for 12 minutes, then top it with a pat of this butter during the last 3 minutes of cooking time. It really infuses fish with a bright, citrus flavour.

THE BEST HOMEMADE APPLE SAUCE

Makes about 950g

Prep time: 10 minutes
Cook time: 25 minutes

Y'all, there is a ton of really good organic apple sauce out there and it is easy to buy it, but there's something about making our own that we really enjoy. We do it as a family and it's become kind of a tradition in the autumn. Some adults dismiss apple sauce as 'baby food', like it's something reserved for kids who are all gums. But you walk into a house where a batch is being made and I guarantee you'll want some, regardless of your age. If you still need an excuse, you can always pair it with pork chops (page 200) or a roasted pork loin (page 80) – but I assure you, real men eat apple sauce straight up.

6 large apples, peeled, cored and cut into chunks (try a mix of Gala and Granny Smith)

240ml apple juice or cider

240ml water

2 cinnamon sticks

$1/4$ teaspoon ground cinnamon

2 tablespoons plus 1 teaspoon granulated sugar

2 tablespoons soft light brown sugar

$1/8$ teaspoon sea salt

pinch of freshly grated nutmeg

Combine the apples, juice or cider, water, cinnamon sticks, cinnamon, sugars, salt and nutmeg in a large saucepan. Bring to the boil over a medium heat, then reduce the heat, cover with a lid and simmer gently for 25 minutes, stirring on occasion, until the apples are extremely soft.

Remove the cinnamon sticks and discard. If you prefer a real smooth apple sauce, you can add the apples and liquid to a blender or food processor and blend until it's the consistency you like best.

Store the apple sauce, covered, in your refrigerator for up to 5 days. Beyond that, you'll want to freeze it.

INGREDIENT NOTES

You can experiment with the kinds of apples you use, making it milder or more tart. Just make sure you use really crisp apples; nothing floury will do.

Want more bang for your buck? Add berries. Adding 115g blueberries to the simmering apples makes this an apple-blueberry sauce.

BROOKE'S BABY FOOD

Brooke saw the first year of our boys' lives as an important opportunity to establish good eating habits. We knew what we didn't want: a battle over food. We didn't want to make four versions of a meal to accommodate picky eaters; likewise, we didn't want to force our children to gag down food they couldn't stomach. We wanted our boys to have a healthy relationship with food – to be willing to try new things and make good choices for themselves.

One of the biggest steps we took towards this goal was making homemade baby food. I've gotta hand it to Brooke, as hard as it was to adjust to having a baby in the house the first time – and then doing it all over again just a couple of years later – she made the time to develop homemade baby food recipes for the boys.

She introduced them to a variety of fruits and vegetables through purées that were more flavourful than the watered-down, mass-produced jars. Her purées tasted more like 'real' food and I swear it's one of the reasons why they're both such good-natured eaters today. We have our battles for sure, but they're not about food. Consequently, dinner is a big part of our day and one that we enjoy together.

Brooke quickly discovered that between the boys' naps, nappy changes and playtimes, it was difficult to carve out even the littlest bit of time to make homemade meals for the toothless. So instead of trying to purée something for the baby every time we were fixing our dinner, she would make big batches of baby food when she had a minute and freeze the extras into ice-cube trays to defrost when she needed them. That's when I realised that mothers in particular are at the mercy of their children's schedule. You can insist on following a schedule all you want, but chances are you won't be the one setting it. Sometimes I'd catch her making food in the middle of the night because one of the boys had

woken her and she couldn't fall back to sleep. That's what parents do: they adapt.

I've also adapted to baby food. When I'm crunched for time in the morning, I take a few of those frozen cubes of sweet potato purée and blend them up, along with a clementine and some ginger, and have myself a fast, satisfying breakfast smoothie. It is surprisingly good.

Today, both of my boys still remember the 'food cubes' Brooke would pull out of the fridge and defrost. At the time, we called 'em 'dinner', but today we call 'em 'popsicles'.

AVOCADO
AND BANANA

Makes 1 ice-cube tray

Prep time: 5 minutes (plus freezing time)
Cook time: zero

Think this sounds like a strange combination? Think again. The banana offers a subtle sweetness to the creamy richness of the avocado. This recipe's got it all: a heavy dose of vitamins and the healthy fats little bodies need.

2 large ripe avocados

1 ripe banana, peeled and sliced

Slice the avocados in half, remove and discard the stones and scoop the flesh into the bowl of a food processor along with the banana. Purée the avocados and banana until they're smooth.

Spoon the mixture into an ice-cube tray and freeze for 4 hours. Pop the cubes out of the tray and place them in freezer bags; label and date. Defrost as needed.

SWEET POTATO
AND APPLE

Makes 1 ice-cube tray

Prep time: 5 minutes (plus freezing time)
Cook time: 15 minutes

Don't wait until your child's teeth come in before he enjoys an apple. By pairing puréed apples with mashed sweet potatoes, you're giving your child something that will taste good and stick to his ribs.

450g sweet potatoes, peeled and cut into 4cm chunks

2 apples, peeled and cut into 4cm chunks

80ml Homemade Chicken Stock (page 205) or water

1/4 teaspoon ground cinnamon (optional; for babies about 8 months old and beyond)

Put 5cm of water in the base of a steamer. Add the sweet potatoes and apples to the basket and steam for about 12 minutes until they're tender. Remove the sweet potatoes and apples to a food processor and purée until smooth. Add the stock or water and pulse to loosen up the mixture just a bit. Season with cinnamon, if using.

Cool the purée to room temperature and then spoon it into an ice-cube tray and freeze for 4 hours. Pop the cubes out of the tray and place them in freezer bags; label and date. Defrost as needed.

GET IN MY STORECUPBOARD

People always ask me what I keep in my storecupboard. I suppose it's like wanting to know how fitness trainers stay in shape, or how Tiger Woods wins so many golf tournaments – we want to know the secret of a person's success.

In my case, there are no secrets in my storecupboard. I don't have a magic elixir that turns plain dishes into something wonderful (unless it's called salt). I do, however, keep my cupboards stocked with some must-haves. If you're new to cooking, consult this list to get yourself prepped before making the recipes in this book. If you're an old hand, check the expiry dates.

STAPLES

Canned beans

Whether it's kidney beans, cannellini beans, chickpeas or pinto beans, I keep a stash around for quick soups, stews, chilli or rice and beans.

Canned tomatoes

When you don't have time to dice 'em fresh, canned tomatoes are a good option for soups, stews, chilli and the like.

Cornflour

This fine, powdery starch is a good thickener. It can be used if your gravy or stew is not thickening up as desired.

Couscous

These tiny granules of durum wheat are really just quick-cooking pasta. Couscous can be used for salads, stuffing vegetables or as a simple side dish on its own.

Creamy peanut butter

Peanuts (which are not nuts but legumes) are a great source of protein, so it's not a big leap to see that this childhood favourite is also nutritious. I keep a jar around for baking or quick after-school snacks – which sometimes is nothing more than a spoonful of the stuff.

Dried fruits

Cranberries, dried figs and raisins are great for dressing up salads.

Long-grain rice, white and brown

The side dish that's always there for you.

Nuts

I like to keep a variety of nuts, stored in airtight containers, to add texture and healthy fats to my recipes. My favourites are pecans, sunflower seeds, salted roasted pistachios, salted roasted almonds and walnuts.

Panko breadcrumbs

I love these extra-crunchy Japanese breadcrumbs.

Pastas

Pasta in the storecupboard pretty much guarantees that you can make *something* for dinner. I always have a variety of shapes and sizes on hand – rigatoni, penne, linguine, wagon wheels, spaghetti – just to keep things interesting.

Pickled cucumber relish

The pickled taste is always a great addition to egg, tuna or my cracker salad (page 25).

Plain flour

This goes without saying. Nonetheless, I'm saying it.

Quick-cooking grits

Not to be mistaken for instant, which don't taste nearly as good, quick-cooking grits can provide a dinner or breakfast in more than 7 but less than 15 minutes.

Sun-dried tomatoes in oil

Why? Because Brooke tosses them in her meatloaf for a dynamite dinner. Always ready; always prepared.

Tomato purée

I always have a can ready to provide a shot here and there for added depth of flavour and an 'umami' boost. (That's a borrowed word from the Japanese that means 'pleasingly savoury taste'.)

Yellow cornmeal

A (Southern) necessity.

CONDIMENTS

Dijon mustard

This condiment, which is a combination of ground mustard and seasonings, provides a strong base for many dressings. It also helps to emulsify, or blend, them.

Hot sauce

This refers to anything that's not Sriracha (see below) but still gets your attention.

Mayonnaise

Sure, it's most commonly used to moisten a sandwich, but a dollop also goes a long way when making creamy dressings.

Soy sauce

Made from fermented soya beans, this salty sauce adds rich flavour to marinades, soups, stews and sauces.

Sriracha sauce

More commonly known as 'rooster sauce' because of the bird on the bottle, this spicy chilli sauce can be added to just about anything for extra heat.

Worcestershire sauce

A dash of this bold-tasting, fermented condiment adds a depth of flavour interest to soups, stews and sauces.

Yellow mustard

Use this fat-free flavour-boosting condiment to top sandwiches or rev up sauces.

OILS

Groundnut oil

This slightly nutty-tasting oil is ideal for frying. It can be safely heated to incredibly high temperatures, and you can cook multiple foods in the same pan of oil because groundnut oil doesn't absorb the flavours of the food.

Olive oil

I use a basic, less expensive olive oil in most of my recipes for sautéeing and roasting.

Extra-virgin olive oil

This high-quality oil is derived from whole, unblemished olives pressed within a day of harvest and has a sharper flavour than regular olive oil. Save this more expensive version for vinaigrettes or for drizzling over a finished dish.

Rapeseed oil

This heart-healthy oil comes from the seeds of the oilseed rape plant. Compared with olive oil, it provides a more neutral taste, making it my all-purpose oil for baking, sautéeing and roasting.

SPICES

Black peppercorns

Peppercorns, which come from dried, immature berries, are my go-to seasoning. I always make sure I have a refill on hand because running out of pepper is like running out of water.

Salt

I use coarse-grain, additive-free kosher salt at home and to prepare all of the recipes in this book. It's easy to handle and adheres to food really well. Sea salt is a good substitute.

SWEETENERS

Listen, sugar, there's a bunch of ways to sweeten up a dish. Here are some of my favourite flavour enhancers that are great to have on hand for pancakes, French toast, hoecakes or to liven up a vinaigrette or roasted vegetables.

Cane /golden syrup

Cane syrup's buttery flavour and golden colour isn't as overpowering as molasses and not as sickly sweet as corn syrup. Sadly, there's only a few cane mills still producing this simple syrup in the USA. Golden syrup is the next best thing.

Caster sugar

Because it dissolves quickly, caster sugar is perfect for sweetening up drinks and cocktails.

Granulated sugar

For all your baking needs. Full stop.

Honey

Many shop-bought versions are made with only a small percentage of real honey, so my family likes to buy local from the farmers' market. You can taste the difference.

Maple syrup

This sticky amber liquid is made from the sap of certain maple trees. Boiling evaporates the water from the otherwise tasteless sap, giving it that familiar sweet flavour.

Soft light brown sugar

The addition of molasses turns white sugar into this soft, slightly caramel-flavoured staple.

VINEGARS

The word 'vinegar' is actually derived from the French term *vin aigre*, which means 'sour wine'. The weak acid, developed through a fermentation process, has literally been around for thousands of years. It has been used as an all-natural cleaning agent and germ killer, but I use it in the kitchen as a base for most dressings and marinades, giving them a clean, flavourful 'bite'. I recommend keeping a bottle of each of the following vinegars on hand; they have subtle but essential differences. None of them are expensive and they seem to last forever – not thousands of years, but pretty close.

Balsamic vinegar

Traditionally made in Italy from unfiltered, unfermented grape juice, this richly coloured dark brown vinegar can cost you a pretty penny if you opt for an aged variety, but inexpensive versions abound.

Cider vinegar

Made from the fermentation of apples and easily identifiable by its caramel colour, cider vinegar adds a touch of colour and bright flavour to recipes.

Red wine vinegar

This variety is made from red wine that is allowed to ferment. And, you guessed it – it's red, which will also affect the colour of your recipes.

White wine vinegar

Like the flavour of wine vinegar, but don't want to mess with the colour of your dressing or marinade? Opt for this clear version made from white wine that also has a somewhat milder taste than the red variety.

SPICE RACK

A good collection of seasonings allows you to spice up any dish, any time. Below is a list of what I keep stocked at home. And as long as you store spices in a cool, dark place, they'll never go bad. They will, however, lose their potency over time. Generally speaking, you can store seasonings for up to six months, so rack 'em up.

Bay leaf

While they look like a herb, bay leaves should be treated like a spice and, as such, perform best when paired with other spices. They're most often found floating lazily in soups.

Cayenne pepper

Not to be confused with chilli powder or paprika, cayenne pepper is a pungent, bright red power derived from a variety of chillies. Because it's more finely ground than dried chilli flakes, it's ideal to whisk into dressings.

Celery seeds

Tiny white celery seeds add a slightly bitter and salty flavour to potato salad and coleslaw.

Chilli powder

Unlike cayenne pepper, which is solely derived from chillies, chilli powder also contains garlic and salt.

Cinnamon

Ever complain that something tastes like tree bark? Well, that's cinnamon for you. The ground brown bark of the cinnamon tree gives a warm, woodsy flavour to any dish, sweet or savoury.

Cumin

Cumin supplies dishes with a nutty, peppery flavour and is most often found in Mexican and Middle Eastern dishes.

Curry powder

Synonymous with South Asian cuisine, curry is actually a combination of several spices that are roasted and ground together, including coriander, cumin, mustard seeds, red and black pepper, fenugreek and turmeric, with possible additions of cinnamon, cloves and cardamom. I love to use curry powder to brighten up chicken, dressings and rice.

Dried chilli flakes

These little flakes pack a hot, smoky flavour. Throw a pinch into a recipe to add heat; just avoid rubbing your eyes afterwards.

Dried oregano

The strong flavour of this herb is more pungent dried than fresh. Add a pinch to liven up rubs, sauces and marinades.

Mustard powder

This powered spice made from the seeds of the mustard plant is a great addition to marinades for beef, pork and other meats.

Garlic powder

Made up of dried, powdered garlic cloves, this seasoning gives dishes a hint of garlic without the chunky texture.

Nutmeg

At one time, this spice was one of the most prized around. Derived from the seed of the nutmeg tree – a tropical evergreen – the strong, sweet flavour pairs particularly well with squashes and lamb.

Old Bay Seasoning

This spice mix has a cult following among purveyors of seafood, though it's also used on poultry and is great sprinkled over fries. While the spice mix is a closely guarded secret, I'd guess it's a blend of cinnamon, ginger, mustard, bay leaves, celery seeds, laurel and black and red pepper. Save yourself the trouble and just buy this brand.

Paprika

Used in the seventies to pretty-up devilled eggs and potato salad, this spice does have a more practical culinary use. Milder than cayenne or dried chilli flakes, paprika adds a palatable kick to dishes without totally knocking you out. The smoked version of this spice is a staple in most Spanish dishes.

CAN'T PUT YOUR FINGER ON IT?

Thanks, y'All

Let's start at the top, shall we? Thank you to Kyle Cathie, the founder of Kyle Books. Kyle reminds me so much of my mother, starting a business and finding her own way to success. I am so thankful and very proud to be a representative of Kyle Books.

Thank you to Anja Schmidt, the lone US employee of Kyle Books. Also a parent in a busy household, she and I really clicked on the direction and tone of our book. Without your guidance, I couldn't have done it.

Thank you to John Kernick and Rizwan Alvi. They are only the top photography team in the business. No big whoop. It was such a pleasure becoming friends with y'all and the result of your work is just beautiful.

A thousand heartfelt thanks to Susie Theodorou and her food styling team, Monica Pierini and Marah Abel. Susie is an artist with food and her work on our book took it to a higher level.

Thanks as well to the rest of the Kyle team: Louise Leffler, Vicki Murrell, Tara O'Sullivan, Nic Jones and David Hearn. Also thanks to Ron Longe for PR guidance.

Thank you to my team at Artist Agency and to my special friend Janis Donnaud, who slid from literary agent to friend about eight years ago. Thank you, Janis, for finding me a wonderful literary home.

Thank you to my two favourite women not named Deen. Brianna Beaudry, who is just the best with recipe development, whether for cookbooks or television shows, and Andrea Goto, who is a masterful writer and knows just the right spot for a comma. We made a hell of a team, ladies.

Thank you to Ray Goto, Andrea's husband, for the illustrations throughout our book. Thank you to Sarah Meighen who, as the perfect assistant, is so important to our family.

Thank you to the City of Savannah, Tybee Island, The University of Georgia, America's Second Harvest and to our friends at Ottawa Farms and Savannah Bee Company for y'all's continued support.

Thank you to my mom, dad, Aunt Peggy and my brother, Bobby, for all being important guiding forces in my life.

And to my wife, Brooke, and our two boys, Jack and Matthew, thank you for y'all's support and the best love and kisses in the whole wide world.

JACK's DEDICATION

To my Mommy,
who I love up the sky.

Rooster's Café
by Jack Deen

FOREWORD BY JAMIE DEEN

Food and family are at the heart of most of my memories, from the time I made my first spaghetti casserole with Momma looking over my shoulder, to the potato salad I've been required to bring to every Christmas since I was old enough to boil an egg. I must've been about eight years old when my mom gave me my first cookbook. I can remember opening up that book and feeling like I'd discovered some secret world – with that book as my guide, I could create something special that people would enjoy.

Both honouring my family's cooking legacy and creating dishes that reflect my personal history have been such a source of happiness for me, but nothing can hold a candle to my greatest creation: my two boys.

My sons inspire and surprise me every single day. Their innocence and kindness motivate me to be the best husband, father and man I can be, and yet I'm still caught off guard when they look at me with love and admiration, because as hard as I try, I constantly worry that I'm gonna mess this parenting thing up. But I felt I got something right the day Jack informed me that he wanted to be a 'cooker man' like me – that he wanted to have a restaurant and write a cookbook of his own. It's the best compliment I could ever get.

As much as I'd like to take all the credit for Jack, the truth is, I owe just as much to his momma. Brooke has had the boys in the kitchen with her pretty much since the day they were born. Together they've blended smoothies, dipped vegetables and baked cookies. Like my mom, Brooke has made the kitchen a place where the family comes together to create something special – be it a dish or a memory.

Jack's Rooster's Café recipes are so much more than a collection of his favourite snacks. It's a collection of his best memories, which is why it's so important to me to include them here. This book – and my life – wouldn't be complete without him, his brother and my wife who brought my boys into the kitchen just like my mom did so many years ago.

A New Chef in the Coop

I've always wanted to grow up to be a 'cooker man' like my daddy. I love helping out on his cooking show when I can, but I also cook at home with my mom. She started letting me help out in the kitchen when I was really little. Mommy and I would play restaurant together. She set up a kitchen for me in the playroom with pots and pans that looked just like the ones in her kitchen, only smaller. I even had a white chef's coat with my name on it. I looked really professional. Together we made frozen fruit smoothies every morning and a healthy snack each afternoon. It wasn't long before I learned to make a whole bunch of recipes. That's when I got the idea to start my own restaurant called Rooster's Café.

Mommy and I spent a whole day planning it out. We made paper menus and covered a table with a chequered tablecloth. I set the table and even put some flowers in a small vase. Mommy folded a paper hat for me – like the ones people wear in old-fashioned ice cream parlours. She wrote 'Rooster's Café' on the side of it.

I called my Ginny and invited her to be the first person to eat at my restaurant. My mom helped me cook cheesy scrambled eggs and Ginny loved it. She even said that one day Rooster's Café would be just as big as her and Daddy's restaurant.

I hope so. But until then, I'll keep practising with my mom. All of my favourite recipes are in this book so you can practise, too. They're easy to make – and even better to eat.

Jack's Breakfast Smoothie

Makes 2 smoothies (225ml each)

Prep time: 5 minutes   Cook time: zero

Making smoothies is one of my favourite things to do. In the summer, my mom and I make them every morning. We pick fruits and vegetables from the little garden we planted. In the winter, I go to the grocery store with my dad and he lets me pick out all different kinds of fruits and vegetables to try together. We always start with yogurt and juice, but after that I get to be creative. I've practised a lot and I think I've come up with the best breakfast smoothie you'll ever taste.

240ml pomegranate juice

120ml low-fat Greek yogurt

75g frozen unsweetened blueberries

160g frozen unsweetened pineapple

1 banana, peeled and cut into chunks

about 1 handful baby spinach

My little brother doesn't like taking medicine. So when he's sick, I make him a smoothie and Dad puts his medicine in it. He drinks it right up!

Add the juice, yogurt, blueberries, pineapple and banana to a blender. Start by blending it on a low speed and work your way up to a higher one. Blend until smooth.

JAMIE'S TIP

I also have a little secret. Don't tell Jack, but there's spinach in this smoothie that's disguised by the colour of the blueberries and pomegranate juice. I pop it in and give it a quick pulse when he's picking out what crazy straw he wants to use. I figure what he doesn't know won't hurt him – in fact, it'll help him.

The Best Cheesy Eggs

Serves 4

Prep time: 5 minutes   Cook time: 5 minutes

The first thing my daddy ever taught me how to make was scrambled eggs. And since I love cheese, we decided to put that in the recipe. Of course, I kept wanting to add more and more cheese and that's when Daddy told me that his Aunt Glyniss used to put chunks of Cheddar in her eggs. We tried it and now I won't even eat eggs unless there are some big nuggets of cheese in there.

8 medium eggs (as fresh as possible, preferably from my Ginny's chickens!)

2 tablespoons sour cream

sea salt and freshly ground black pepper

30g butter

30g mature Cheddar cheese (or your favourite cheese), grated

35g mature Cheddar cheese, cubed

Crack the eggs into a large bowl and whisk them together until they're smooth, yellow and foamy. Add the sour cream and whisk until well mixed. Season the eggs with just a pinch of salt and pepper.

Heat a large non-stick frying pan over a medium heat. Add the butter and, once it's melted and foamy, add the eggs. Let the eggs sit for about 30 seconds, then turn the heat to medium and stir constantly for 3–4 minutes with a rubber spatula until creamy wet curds form. Remove from the heat and carefully stir in the cheeses, folding the eggs over on top of themselves.

JAMIE'S TIP

The key to delicious eggs is to not overcook them. You've got to remove them from the heat when they still look a little wet.

Bird-in-a-Nest

Serves 1

Prep time: 5 minutes   Cook time: 10 minutes

This is one of my favourite breakfasts that Dad makes for me on a school day. He lets me cut the shape out of the centre of the bread and it's really fun seeing the egg cook into that shape. And the best part is, if we're running really late, I can take it with me.

1 slice bread of your choosing

30g butter

1 medium egg

sea salt and freshly ground black pepper

1 slice your favourite cheese (optional)

Use a cookie cutter (stars and hearts are fun!) or a round glass to stamp out a hole in the centre of your bread.

Melt the butter in a non-stick frying pan over a medium heat until it's foamy. Add the bread to the pan, then crack the egg into the hole in the centre of the bread. Season the egg with a small pinch of salt and pepper. Cook for 3½ minutes until the toast is golden brown and the egg is beginning to set, then flip and cook the other side for 3 minutes more. (Top your bread with a slice of cheese during the last minute of cooking if you want to make it cheesy.)

JAMIE'S TIP

This is the lazy man's French toast, or what I like to call the 'beat-the-late-bell breakfast'.

Apple Sauce Muffins

Makes 12 muffins

Prep time: 5 minutes   Cook time: 25 minutes

When I was in pre-school, my teacher sent all of the kids home with a recipe for apple sauce muffins to make with their parents. Dad and I made it together and it was OK, then he came up with this recipe and it's A+ OK.

250g plain flour

160g soft light brown sugar

2 teaspoons baking powder

½ teaspoon bicarbonate of soda

1¼ teaspoons ground cinnamon

½ teaspoon sea salt

240g unsweetened apple sauce

120ml rapeseed oil

2 medium eggs, lightly beaten

130g walnuts, chopped

Preheat the oven to 180°C/gas mark 4. Line a 12-cup muffin tin with paper cases.

Whisk together the flour, sugar, baking powder, bicarbonate of soda, cinnamon and salt in a large bowl. In a medium bowl, whisk together the apple sauce, oil and eggs.

Make a well in the centre of the dry ingredients and add the wet ingredients. Stir the batter until it's barely combined and then stir in the walnuts, being careful not to overmix. Using an ice cream scoop, spoon the batter into the muffin cups. Bake for 25 minutes until the muffins are springy and a skewer inserted into the centre comes out clean. Leave to cool before serving.

Almond Crunch Mix

Makes 380g

Prep time: 5 minutes   Cook time: zero

When my friends come over to play, I mix all of my favourite cereals, nuts and dried fruit into a big bowl. Whenever we get hungry for a snack, I can pour some into little bags and we can get back to having fun.

30g Shreddies

140g roasted almonds

55g high-fibre crunch cereal

60g dried cherries or cranberries

60g dried mango, chopped

35g salted roasted sunflower seeds

Mix everything up in a bowl. Store in an airtight storage jar.

JAMIE'S TIP

If you're having friends over and they have kids in tow, this is a great snack mix to hold everyone off while the dinner is cooking.

Caramel Apples

Serves 6

Prep time: 5 minutes (plus 30 minutes chilling)
Cook time: 5 minutes

Every time I visit one of the sweet shops in town, I go straight to the case that holds the huge gooey caramel apples covered in all sorts of good things, like nuts, pieces of sweets and even cookie crumbs. I just had to make one for myself, and it turns out that it's really easy to do. Just be sure to have an adult help you because the melted caramel is real hot – but have them make their own apple because you aren't going to want to share.

6 organic apples of your choosing

1 tablespoon distilled white vinegar

6 lollipop sticks

400g individually wrapped caramels

3 tablespoons full-fat milk

toppings: toffee pieces, crushed cookies, chopped pecan nuts

Line a baking tray with greaseproof paper. Give the apples a nice bath in cold water with a splash of white vinegar, which helps the caramel stick to the apples. Dry them off really well with a clean tea towel. Use scissors to snip out the apple stalks. Insert a stick into the top of each apple.

Unwrap the caramels and place them in a large microwave-safe bowl. Add the milk and microwave for 3 minutes. Give the caramels a stir, then microwave again for a further 2 minutes until they are completely melted. Leave the caramel mixture to cool down for 1–2 minutes.

Dip each apple into the caramel, twirling the stick to make sure the apple gets completely coated. Straight away, sprinkle the caramel apple with toppings, pressing them gently to stick, then set it on the prepared tray. Refrigerate for 30 minutes until they're set.

Peanut Butter and Jam Thumbprint Cookies

Makes 15 cookies

Prep time: 15 minutes   Cook time: 15 minutes

This cookie is really fun to make with my mom because I get to play with my food. After she mixes all the ingredients together, I drop the dough onto the baking tray, flatten it with a fork and press my thumbprint in the centre to make a little well that I can fill with jam. All of my friends like to eat these, too. What kid doesn't like peanut butter and jam?

260g crunchy peanut butter

55g soft light brown sugar

50g granulated sugar

1 medium egg, at room temperature

1 teaspoon pure vanilla extract

strawberry jam

Preheat the oven to 180°C/gas mark 4. Line a baking tray with baking parchment.

Beat together the peanut butter, brown sugar, granulated sugar, egg and vanilla in a large bowl until fluffy. Spoon heaped tablespoons of batter onto the prepared baking tray about 4cm apart. Flatten with a fork. Use your thumb to make a 2cm indent in the centre of each cookie (being sure not to break through to the other side). Spoon ½ teaspoon of jam into each 'thumbprint'. Bake for 12 minutes until golden. Leave the cookies to cool on a wire rack completely before serving.

Monkey Snack

Makes 1 sandwich

Prep time: 5 minutes
Cook time: zero

My dad comes up with the craziest ideas, but this is probably one of my favourites. When we were out of hot dogs but had a whole bag of rolls, Dad looked around the kitchen, saw some ripe bananas and said, 'I got it!' He smeared the roll with peanut butter and jam and then set a whole banana inside, inventing what we call a Monkey Snack. It's the greatest sandwich of all time.

1 hot dog roll

smooth peanut butter

strawberry jam

1 banana, peeled

Spread the inside of the roll with peanut butter and jam. Add the banana like you would a hot dog. Enjoy!

You definitely need a grown-up to help you with the PB&J cookies because you need to use a mixer and a hot oven.

Fun-fetti Cupcakes

Makes 12 cupcakes

Prep time: 5 minutes   Cook time: 25 minutes

I'm all about cupcakes, and the more sprinkles, the better. Besides, without a heap of sprinkles it's just plain ol' cake – and what's the fun in that?

120ml canola oil

150g sugar

2 medium eggs

120ml sour cream

1 teaspoon pure vanilla extract

190g plain flour

1½ teaspoons baking powder

½ teaspoon fine sea salt

40g rainbow sprinkles, plus more for topping

cream cheese frosting (recipe follows)

Preheat the oven to 180°C/gas mark 4. Line a standard 12-cup cupcake tin with paper cases.

Add the oil and sugar to a large bowl and whisk really well for about 2 minutes until blended. (You may need to ask an adult for a hand with this one – little arms tire pretty fast.) Whisk in the eggs, one at a time, then the sour cream and then the vanilla.

Whisk together the flour, baking powder and salt in a medium bowl. Add the dry ingredients to the wet ones and stir them until they're blended. Add the sprinkles and give a few good stirs, being careful not to overmix or you'll have tie-dye streaked cupcakes – but if you do, who cares? That's fun, too!

Divide the batter between the cupcake cases and place the tin on a baking tray. Bake the cupcakes for about 22 minutes until they're puffed and golden (a skewer inserted into the centre should come out clean). Leave the cupcakes to cool completely before frosting.

To decorate the cupcakes, use a knife to spread the tops with frosting and top with more sprinkles.

Cream Cheese Frosting

Makes 625g (enough for 12 cupcakes)

Prep time: 5 minutes   Cook time: zero

270g icing sugar

350g cream cheese, at room temperature

1 teaspoon pure vanilla extract

your favourite gel food colourings

Whisk the sugar in a bowl to break up any lumps. There's nothing worse than lumpy frosting!

Add cream cheese to a large bowl and beat it with an electric hand mixer until it's light and fluffy. Gradually sprinkle in the sugar, then add the vanilla and beat until it's fully blended. Divide the frosting between small bowls and stir in the gel food colouring, mixing until you get the colours you want.

Frozen Chocolate Bananas

Serves 4

Prep time: 20 minutes (plus freezing time)
Cook time: 5 minutes

Kind of like the ice-lolly stand I want to start up, Dad told me that when he was young, he wanted to move to the Bahamas and sell frozen chocolate bananas with all sorts of different toppings, like sprinkles and nuts. He says it every time we make them, which makes me think he might just do it one day.

2 medium bananas

4 chopsticks

225g milk chocolate, chopped, or milk chocolate chips

2 teaspoons rapeseed oil

chopped peanuts or rainbow sprinkles (optional)

Line a baking tray with greaseproof paper. Peel the bananas, then cut them in half. Insert the chopsticks halfway into the cut end of the bananas. Place the bananas on the prepared tray and freeze for 45 minutes.

To melt the chocolate, add the chocolate to a small glass bowl and place over a saucepan of simmering water (making sure the bottom doesn't touch the water). Stir until melted, then whisk in the oil and remove from the heat.

Dip and turn the frozen bananas into the chocolate, making sure they get completely covered. (You will need to spoon some chocolate on the bananas.) Let the extra chocolate drip off, then sprinkle with the chopped peanuts or sprinkles. Place the coated bananas back on the tray and freeze for 30 minutes until the chocolate sets.

My dad says he might have written up a business plan at some point. Whatever that means.

Watermelon Kiwi Pops

Makes 6 pops

Prep time: 5 minutes (plus 4 hours freezing time)   Cook time: zero

Mom and I make ice lollies (we call them Popsicles in the USA) together all the time. I thought we could open an ice-lolly stand at the beach during summertime and make some money selling them. I'm pretty sure this refreshing recipe would be a bestseller.

2 kiwi fruits, peeled and sliced

6 ice-lolly moulds

450g deseeded watermelon, cubed

50g caster sugar (optional)

Place two slices of kiwi fruit into each ice-lolly mould. Combine the watermelon and sugar (if your watermelon isn't sweet enough) in a blender and purée until smooth. Fill the ice-lolly moulds and freeze them for about 4 hours until they're firm.

Peanut-Butter Apple Core

Serves 1

Prep time: 5 minutes   Cook time: zero

When I'm at home, I like to take apples that my mom cuts up and dip them in peanut butter. When I asked Dad if he could pack apples and peanut butter as a snack for school, he came up with this idea. He cores an apple, fills it with peanut butter and puts it in a plastic bag so that I can take it to school. I like it because it looks like an ordinary old apple on the outside, but I can eat my way through the whole thing – even the peanut-butter core.

1 apple of your choosing, well washed and dried

65g smooth peanut butter

Carefully use an apple corer/wedger to cut the apple into even wedges and remove the core. Fill the space where the core was with the peanut butter and close up the apple slices around it.

JAMIE'S TIP

I know Jack likes this because it's messy, but it's also good for him. It makes a great portable apple and peanut butter snack – just wrap up in a to-go container and you're off.

S'More Ice Cream Sandwiches

Makes 6 sandwiches

Prep time: 5 minutes (plus 30 minutes freezing time)   Cook time: zero

I love roasting marshmallows. My dad and I see who can cook theirs the longest without it catching on fire or falling off the stick. One summer, my friends wanted to roast marshmallows, but Dad said it was too hot for a fire, so he came up with this warm-weather s'more made with ice cream. I leave the hot fudge off mine because I don't like chocolate, but everyone else seems to really like it.

300g vanilla ice cream

12 digestive biscuits

210g jar Marshmallow Fluff

175g jarred chocolate fudge sauce, hot (the thick kind you microwave to loosen up)

Leave the ice cream out on your worktop for 30 minutes to soften it up. Spread one digestive biscuit with the Marshmallow Fluff and another with the hot fudge sauce.

Once the ice cream is soft, place 1 scoop of ice cream onto the marshmallow side of the digestive biscuit and spread the ice cream to the edges. Sandwich the two biscuits together. Repeat with the remaining biscuits, Fluff, fudge and ice cream. Freeze the ice cream sandwiches for 30 minutes, or until firm and ready to serve.

JAMIE'S TIP

Fancier palates can substitute a chocolate-hazelnut spread for the hot fudge.

Homemade Clay

Makes about 950g of clay

Prep time: 5 minutes   Cook time: 5 minutes

My parents are constantly reminding me to pick up my toys so that my little brother doesn't put them in his mouth – and believe me, he eats everything. That's the nice thing about this homemade clay; it's something Matthew and I can play with together because it's safe to eat (though I don't recommend it because it doesn't taste very good). Now if I can only teach him not to grind it into Mom's white carpet . . .

250g plain flour

190g sea salt

1 tablespoon cream of tartar

475ml water

2 tablespoons vegetable oil

your favourite gel food colourings

Whisk together the flour, salt and cream of tartar in a medium saucepan. Stir in the water and oil, then turn the heat to medium. Cook, stirring, for about 5 minutes until the dough comes away from the sides of the pan. The dough gets thick as it cooks.

Remove the clay from the pan and leave it to cool for about 3 minutes until it's just warm to the touch. Knead the dough until it becomes really smooth, then divide it into as many colours as you want. To add colour, knead in the colouring. Store each colour of clay in a separate airtight container.

JAMIE'S TIP

This is messy, y'all. If you'd rather not get covered in food colouring, place the dough in plastic bags before adding the gel and kneading it.

Ants on a Log

I first saw this recipe on a kid's show on TV and thought it looked like something I could do. I went to my dad and asked if we could try to make it together. As long as you have an adult cut the celery for you, this is a real easy recipe. The hardest part is getting the peanut butter onto the celery. It can get a little messy, but Dad says that's all part of cooking.

celery sticks

smooth peanut butter

raisins (or other dried fruit like cranberries or chopped mango)

Trim the celery into 7.5cm-long pieces. Spread some peanut butter down the centre hollow of the celery and dot with raisins or other dried fruit.

JAMIE'S TIP

We've got red fire ants around here, so I like to give Jack's recipe a Southern spin by substituting dried cranberries for the raisins.

Peanut Butter Balls

Makes 16 treats

Prep time: 15 minutes (plus chilling time)
Cook time: zero

My Ginny told me that she used to make Peanut Butter Balls all the time when she was a little girl, so she was really excited to teach me how to make them for myself. And because there's no cooking, we can do it straight after school for a quick, healthy snack that tastes really good.

260g smooth peanut butter
75g dried skimmed milk
85g honey

Stir together the peanut butter, dried milk and honey in a large bowl. The mixture will be very thick, so you may have to use some muscles. Once it's all blended together, roll the dough into walnut-sized balls. Place the balls on a baking tray and put it in the fridge for 20 minutes so that the cookies get nice and firm.